How Passion
―― CAN MAKE ――
A Business

MARTIN VAN HELDEN

How Passion Can Make A Business

Copyright © Martin Van Helden 2023

The Author has asserted their rights under the Copyright Act 1968 (the Act) to be identified as the author of this work.

All rights reserved. No part of this publication may be reproduced, stored in a retrieval system, or transmitted in any form or by any means, electronic, mechanical, photocopying, recording or otherwise, without the prior written permission of the author. Any person who does any unauthorised act in relation to this publication may be liable to criminal prosecution and civil claims for damages.

The Australian Copyright Act 1968 (the Act) allows a maximum of one chapter or ten per cent of this book, whichever is the greater, to be photocopied for educational purposes by an educational institution holding a statutory education licence provided that the educational institution (or body that administers it) has given a remuneration notice to the Copyright Agency (Australia) under the Act.

ISBN: 978-1-922784-79-7 (Paperback)

 A catalogue record for this book is available from the National Library of Australia

Self-Published by Martin Van Helden with assistance by Clark & Mackay

Proudly printed in Australia by Clark & Mackay

CONTENTS

Introduction 13

Chapter 1   Does Your Surroundings
            (Environment) Make A Difference?...................... 17
Your Environment Can Be A Source Of Motivation 17
You Need To Create A Favorable Physical Environment.... 17
Find Inspiration From Within Your Community 18
Build Connections With Other Professionals 19
Surround Yourself With Successful People 19
Have A Network Of Supporters 19
Consider Technology 20
Incorporate Self-Care Techniques Into Your
Business Routine.. 20
Stay Motivated Even In The Face Of Challenges 21
Make It Fun!... 22
The Impact Of Business Ideology And
Personal Opinions On Opportunities................................... 22
Understanding The Balance Of Professionalism
& Personal Opinion... 23
Knowing Your Customer Is Essential
To Business Success 24
Being Flexible & Open-Minded Can
Lead To More Opportunities 25
Embracing A Growth Mindset Can Repair
Mistakes & Open You Up To Better Prospects...................... 25
Narrow-Minded Belief: A Hindrance
To Business Opportunity... 27
Understand That Traditional Business
Models Can Limit Growth 27
Evaluate The Evidence For Or Against A New Idea............. 28
Understand That New Ideas Can Solve Old Problems 28

- Identify Areas For Improvement 29
- The Art Of Risk Assessment: Knowing When To Take The Leap 29
- Evaluate Pros And Cons 30
- Research 30
- Harness Creativity And Innovation 31

Chapter 2   Not Today, I Will Do It Tomorrow 33
- Lack Of Passion Gives Birth To Procrastination 33
- How Can Lack Of Passion Lead To Procrastination? 33
  - Lack Of Excitement 34
  - Incorrect Prioritization 34
  - Fixed Mindset 34
- The Emotional And Psychological Effects Of A Lack Of Passion 35
  - 1. Emotional Impact 35
  - 2. Cognitive Impact 35
- How Do You Get Out Of This Mess? 36
  - Get Excited About What You're Doing 36
  - Remind Yourself Of Your Purpose 36
  - Break It Down Into Smaller Tasks 36
  - Reflect And Identify Your Goals 36
  - Prioritize Tasks 37
  - Make Good Use Of Your Time 37
- A Change Of Environment Can Help You Focus 38
  - Change Your Environment 40
  - Go For Breaks 40
  - Use Technology 40
- Add Color And Decor 41
  - Invest In Good Lighting 42
  - Add Some Greenery 42
- Utilizing Rewards To Achieve Goals 42
- What Are The Benefits Of Implementing Rewards? 44
  - Motivation 44
  - Positive Reinforcement 44
  - Focusing & Habits Formation 44

How To Set Up Effective Reward Systems 45
    Define Your Goals... 45
    Set Those Rewards 45
    Keep Track Of Progress 45
What Should You Avoid?.. 46
    Don't Use Incentives For Everything............................... 46
    Don't Overdo It.. 46
    Avoid Negative Consequences... 47
Using Progress Notes To Monitor Personal Tasks................ 47
Why Create Progress Notes?.. 48
    Things To Note... 49
    Making Adjustments In Real Time 49
    First Note Down All Your Progress 49
    Establish Milestones And Goals....................................... 50
    Be Flexible With Adjustments.. 50

Chapter 3   Confidence Is The Base
                    For All Your Outcomings............................... 51
Doing Just What You Already Love Boosts Confidence...... 51
What Does It Mean To Do What You Like?.......................... 51
Understanding The Benefits Of Doing What You Like 52
Identifying Your Preferences And Interests 53
How Do You Handle Self-Doubt
While Doing What You Love?.. 54
    So Recognize Imposter Syndrome................................... 54
    Build Yourself Up With Positive Affirmations............... 54
Confident People Are Always Going To Succeed
In Business... 56
What Does It Mean To Be Confident?................................... 56
Benefits Of An Increased Sense Of Self-Confidence 57
    Growth Opportunities... 58
    A Positive Attitude... 58
    Inspire Others... 58
Strengthening Your Resilience To
Overcome Challenges 58

Keys To Developing A Greater Sense Of
Self-Confidence 59
    Acknowledging Your Good Qualities 59
    Knowing Your Weaknesses 59
    Establishing Goals 60
    Celebrating Achievements 60
Common Mistakes Made By
Unconfident People In Business 60
    Not Taking Risks 60
    Not Taking Feedback Constructively 60
    Not Being Open Minded 61

**Chapter 4   Find Out About Yourself In Relation
With Your Mission** 63
Your Field Of Expertise Should Determine
What You Do 63
What Are The Benefits Of Specialization? 63
Defining Your Skills And Areas Of Expertise 64
Making Opportunities To Develop Your Expertise 64
Differentiating Between Tasks That Should
Be Outsourced And Those You Should Take On 65
    Your Skillset 66
    Your Resources 66
Why Hiring Professionals Is Also Essential To
Specialization 66
Setting Goals That Encourage Your Skill Development 67
Don't Get Into A Business You Don't Understand 68
Identifying The Risks Of Launching A Business Without
Sufficient Knowledge 69
Staying Informed And Being Able To Anticipate
Changes In The Industry 70
Need To Protect Yourself With Proper Legal Advice 70
    Why Get Legal Advice? 71

Chapter 5 Stay Focused 73
How An Entrepreneur Can Apply
Focus For Business Success 73
Understanding What Focus Is And
Why It Is Important 73
The Benefits Of Having A Focused Mindset 74
Setting Achievable Goals 74
Growing Your Network Wisely... 75
    Finding Your Tribe 75
Develop An Action Plan And Accountability System.......... 76
    Create An Action Plan.. 76
    Hold Yourself Accountable 76
    Find Support Resources 76
Optimizing Time Management Habits And Practices......... 77
    Set A Schedule 77
    Establish Rules For Interruptions 77
    Stick To Deadlines 77
The Bottom Up Focus System: How It Can
Help You Achieve Your Goals... 78
Exploring The Basics Of The Bottom Up Focus System....... 78
Identifying Your Goals 79
Breaking Down Goals Into Bite-Sized Pieces 79
Setting An Action Plan For Your Goals 80
Monitoring Your Progress And Making Adjustments 81
The Pattern Of Celebrating Success
And Gaining Momentum... 82
Golf: A Subtle Mystery Of Business Focus.......................... 83
Can The Sport Help Improve Focus And Concentration?.. 84
The Parallels Between Golf And Business Strategy 84

Chapter 6 Learn From Experience............................. 87
Success Is Hidden In Past Failures 87
Identifying Your Past Failures 87
Uncovering The Lessons Learned From Your Failures........ 88
Contemplating How Your Failures Have
Helped Shape Who You Are Today...................................... 88

Reflection And Evaluation 89
Embracing Failure 89
Re-Framing Your Perspective To Find
Success In Failures 89
Breaking Down The Barriers Of Fear
In Order To Take Risks 90
Moving Forward Towards Success
With A Fresh Mindset 91
The Importance Of Perseverance And Resilience 94
Staying Positive In The Face Of Failure 94
Don't Be Discouraged By Failure 95
Learn From Your Mistakes 95
Think Outside The Box 95

Chapter 7   Make A New Flexible Plan And
            Adjust It As You Move On 103
The Advantage Of Flexible Business Plans 103
What Is A Flexible Business Plan? 103
Benefits Of Having A Flexible Business Plan 104
Identifying Gaps In Traditional Business Plans 104
Lack Of Agility 105
Limited Creativity 105
Insufficient Feedback Loops 105
Strategies For Implementing A Flexible Business Plan 106
Set Organizational Goals 106
Monitor Your Progress 106
Involve Teams & Customers 106
What Can You Do To Ensure Your Plan
Stays Flexible? 106
Prioritize Agility 107
Review Regularly 107
Leverage Technology 107
What Are The Common Pitfalls
With Flexible Business Plans? 107
Being Overly Optimistic 107
Not Creating Enough Structure 108

Too Rigid 108
A Lesson From Popular Businesses
Which Failed Due To Rigid Business Plans 109
Kodak: Mistaking The Market For A Camera 109
Blockbuster: Ignoring Streaming Video 110
 Refusal To Adapt 110
 Lost Customers 111
Nokia: Refusing To Adapt To Smartphones 111
Borders: Misjudging Its Customers' Needs 111
Myspace: Overlooking Social Media Trends 112

Chapter 8 Head For The Finish, Not For The Door 115
The Relevance Of Time Management To
Achieving Set Goals 115
 The Importance Of Setting Realistic Goals 118
 Optimizing The Work Environment 119
 Helpful Time Management Tools 121
 Overcoming The "Goal Killer" - Procrastination 122
 Deal With Perfection 123
Patience And Persistence For Business Success:
The Winning Combination 124
 Why Are They Important In Business? 124
 The Power Of Delayed Gratification 127
 Overcoming The Unavoidable: Obstacles And
 Setbacks 127
 Fears Hold You Back From Embracing Failure 132
 The Power Of A Growth Mindset 133
 Strategies For Learning From Mistakes
 And Moving Forward 134

Chapter 9 Why Don't You Get A Job? 137
Before You Get That Job 137
 The Effects Of Staying In A Job
 That Does Not Satisfy You 138
 How A Stagnant Career Affects Personal Life 139

How A Stagnant Career Affects
　　Your Financial Stability 140
　　Does It Have Any Impact On Your
　　Professional Development? 140
　Why You Should Consider Owning A Business 143
　　• Flexibility And Work-Life Balance 145
　　• Unlimited Income Potential 145
　　• Freedom To Pursue Passion Projects 146
　　• Control Over Business Decisions 147
　　• Sense Of Accomplishment 147
　　• Opportunities For Personal
　　 And Professional Growth 148
　　• Tax Benefits Of Being A Business Owner 149
　　• Building A Legacy For Future Generations 149

Chapter 10　Get A Mentor 151
　The Power Of Mentorship: Why You
　Need A Mentor To Grow Your Business 151
　　What Is Mentorship And Why Is It Important? 151
　　Types Of Mentorship 153
　　Steps To Finding The Right Mentor 154
　　What To Expect From Your Business Mentor 156
　　How Do You Incorporate Mentorship
　　Into Your Overall Business Strategy? 158
　　Key Takeaways For Entrepreneurs
　　Seeking Business Mentors 158
　Collaboration Over Competition: Growing Your
　Business Through Idea Exchange With Niche Partners. ... 159
　　Understanding Niche Partnership? 160
　　The Difference Between Collaboration And
　　Competition 161
　　Benefits Of Exchanging Ideas With Niche Partners 162
　　Identifying Potential Niche
　　Partners For Collaboration 163
　　Best Practices For Successful Collaboration
　　With Niche Partners 165

Measure The Success Of Niche Partnerships 165

Chapter 11 Take On People With Skills 169
Your Business Needs Highly Skilled And
Passionate Workers 169
    The Importance Of Skill In The Workplace 170
    How To Identify Highly Skilled And
    Passionate Workers 172
    How Do You Foster Passion And Skill
    Development In Your Workforce? 173
    Strategies For Creating A Passion-
    Driven Work Environment 174
    Examples Of Brand Reaping These Benefits 175

**Chapter 12 How Can We Do This
Instead Of I Can't Do This** 179
How Optimism Can Help You Achieve
Your Goals: The Science Behind Positive Thinking 179
    Optimism Vs. Pessimism: The Differences
    And How They Affect Your Goal Achievement 181
    The Role Of Self-Talk: How Your Inner
    Dialogue Can Affect Your Mindset And Goals 183
    Overcoming Obstacles With Optimism 183
    Visualization: How Imagining Success
    Can Help You Achieve Goals 184
    Gratitude: A Channel To Optimism And Goal
    Achievement 185
    What The Combination Of Optimism
    And Resilience Can Do 186

Chapter 13 Have The Passion And Have Success 189
    Drawing Inspiration From The Ray Croc Story 189
    Who Is Ray Kroc? 189
    The Early Life Of Ray Kroc And His Struggles 190
    How Ray Kroc Discovered "Think And Grow Rich" ... 192

How Ray Kroc Turned A Small Burger
Restaurant Into A Global Empire 192
Did You See Persistence And Determination
In Ray Kroc's Success Story? 193
The Leadership Style And Business
Philosophy That Helped Ray Kroc 194
His Challenges And How He Overcame Them 194
His Legacy And Impact On The
Fast-Food Industry 195
Lessons From Ray Kroc's Journey From
Reading "Think And Grow Rich" To
Becoming A Global Business Owner 196
What Have You Learned From Ray Croc,
The Man Behind The Success Of Mcdonald? 197

Conclusion 199
About the Author 203

INTRODUCTION

At its core, passion is a strong emotion towards something that inspires and motivates you. It's something that drives your creativity and helps you maintain focus in order to see your ideas come to life. Without it, it can be hard to summon the motivation or the energy needed to really get things done.

Without passion, there's a lack of excitement towards a project or goal. You can no longer connect with it on an emotional level, so the enthusiasm for seeing it through wanes. This can lead to procrastination - especially when tasks become overwhelming - because there's not enough enthusiasm left to push through them.

What's more, procrastination can be incredibly damaging because it leads to deadlines being missed and goals left unaccomplished. It's important then to maintain your passion for what you do and keep in mind why you chose this project in the first place. That way you'll be able to stay motivated and achieve your goals more easily.

Success often occur when you engage in what you love. If your hobby becomes your business, it becomes very easy to do such a business as you may never get bored. The fact that it is your area of interest is enough to keep you going. A person who naturally talks a lot and goes into TV broadcasting will have a higher tendency of remaining in the trade during challenging times than a person who does not have the habit of talking. You may want to ask "Why?" Where else could the person function better? Think about that. They can become 'actors' in any other discipline. But they know they have a comparative advantage over others in talking, so they would rather face the storm than quit.

If what you love doing is your passion, then it is only true to say that you don't get bored easily when you start it. It's your life - I mean your source of inspiration. Some people, while at work, often prefer to use their leisure to do what they love. For some people, it is football; for others, it is writing. Just imagine if those things were their actual jobs. What level of productivity do you think they would exhibit?

To succeed in business just like in achieving personal goals, it is important you consider taking on your areas of interest - the very things you have passion for. Passion can be your motivator when everything around you seems not to be working. Our dreams of becoming successful in life or in business will become reality when we venture into what we love. It doesn't have to be a regular hobby like singing, traveling or playing games; it can be a more technical things like caring for sick people, counseling people, and all of that. Just do what you love and you'll be surprised how quickly you'll get to the top.

Men like Henry Ford of Ford, Sir Richard Branson of Virgin Atlantic, Steve Jobs of Apple, legendary Tony Robbins of Tony Robbins Productions; and a couple other people you find in your homeland built their businesses on passion.

They succeeded because they are 'powerful'. What power? Passion. Get it involved in a business and nothing will be able to stop you!

One thing cannot be untrue: failure is vital for growth and eventual success. Don't be afraid of it. Those successful guys you know may not tell you - they had once failed at some points. What distinguishes them from those that utterly failed? They never allowed the failures to weigh them down. That's the secret!

Again, your surroundings or environment can either open you to beautiful ideas that help you succeed or keep you in ignorance and mental darkness. Cultivate the habit of moving into spaces (environment) where you get inspired. It's a great tool to succeed in life and business. Do it as often as possible and never get tired until you attain success.

In this book I will highlight some things to think about that helped me to set up and own several businesses, which have been helpful for several people who currently work for me. You have to seek knowledge about success and successful people, to achieve success. I am experienced in this field and I know that knowledge gathering is a necessary part of business. It never stops but keeps going until your business gets better. I spent countless hours reading books about how my businesses could grow. I tested many of the theories I learned on myself (and unknowingly on people around me), until I filtered what works from what doesn't.

One thing I have decided to dedicate my life to is to help people get the most out of their business and life, generally. Life becomes meaningful when you are sure of a rewarding future - yours and that of your family; and when you have all the necessary resources to take you there.

Passion was what inspired me to start the businesses I had owned, and that is why they still thrive! Even under new management.

You can benefit of from my wealth of experience as I will outline in this book a few things you can take to your advance, that would require no further research. Just follow the steps here and we will meet at the top to talk about your success story too!

Chapter 1

Does Your Surroundings (Environment) Make a Difference?

Your Environment Can Be a Source of Motivation

To succeed in business, there's no one-size-fits-all approach. Everyone needs their own unique formula for success, one that helps them reach their goals and drives them to do more. But the environment where we work is often overlooked as an important factor in this equation.

Your surroundings can be a powerful tool for cultivating passion in your business endeavors - even when your motivation starts to flounder. But it's important to understand how and why your environment can have such an impact on your enthusiasm for work and success. But you need to ask yourself some critical questions. How can you use the space around you, from where you live to how you organize your desk, as a way of reigniting passion in your professional life?

You Need to Create a Favorable Physical Environment

Having an environment that inspires and supports you is key to being successful in any business. The physical environment you work in can have a huge impact on your motivation, and the level of success you achieve. Creating a positive workspace can help you stay focused and inspired while enabling you to reach new heights of success.

But how do you ignite your passion for business success through your physical environment?

- Set up an area that is free from distractions. Eliminating all possible distractions will help you stay focused on the task at hand and not get sidetracked.
- Play motivating music. Listening to upbeat music can help boost your energy and inspire productivity.
- Get organized. Having an organized workspace helps create clarity, which can in turn lead to better decision making.
- Allow for creativity. Having creative elements such as inspiring art pieces or plants around your workplace can help spur creative solutions and ideas.
- Utilize natural light and keep windows open when possible. Vitamin D from natural sunlight can help boost energy levels while fresh air helps clear concentration fogging mental fatigue that could affect productivity levels.

Find Inspiration from Within Your Community

No matter where you are, there are people and situations around you that can help you find your passion for business success. Your environment is full of stories, histories and a wealth of experiences which can be used to inspire you and to make sure that your success continues long into the future. Start by looking within your community - who do you know who has achieved something extraordinary in the field of business? Talk to them, learn from them and digest their advice. Take a look at how they achieved success and see how their story applies to your own journey.

Then look at the businesses in your area - take a look at their successes, failures and trends. What do these businesses have that you don't? Or what could be improved? How do they stay competitive within their markets? Learning from their experiences can help shape the decisions that you make for your own business.

But don't forget to look at yourself; use self-assessment techniques such as journaling or goal-setting to pinpoint areas where improvement is needed. It is up to you to take the necessary steps towards achieving success in business. Taking control of your own destiny will reignite passion for what lies ahead.

Build Connections With Other Professionals

You don't have to work alone to achieve success. You can increase your business success by connecting with other entrepreneurs, professionals and mentors in the same field as you. Building relationships with people who are looking to learn and grow alongside you can be immensely valuable for your own development as well as for the growth of your business.

Surround Yourself with Successful People

The saying "you become who you surround yourself with" rings especially true in business. If you want to succeed, surround yourself with only those who find success. Great minds think alike, and that can include business-minded people who understand the importance of goal setting, hard work and dedication on the journey towards success. Interact with these individuals regularly, and they can help ignite passion in you when it might be waning.

Have a Network of Supporters

Having an experienced mentor is a great way to gain valuable knowledge - but it may not always be feasible or practical depending on what stage you're at in your own business journey. Instead, connecting and networking with peers gives you access to support, advice and general encouragement - all of which are essential ingredients in reaching those goals of your own businesses pursuits.

This type of support network also provides a platform where ideas can be exchanged which can help open up new opportunities for progression or expansion that weren't possible previously. Plus, having a group of like-minded professionals around you takes away some of the pressure from coming up with ideas or finding solutions by yourself - so it could also act as a creative sounding board for potential opportunities too.

Consider Technology

Technology has opened up so many possibilities for entrepreneurs. It can help you explore new business opportunities and connect with potential partners and customers more easily. It's also great for networking and collaboration, keeping in contact with current customers, and learning from successful entrepreneurs.

That said, technology also comes with its own set of challenges. You need to be prepared to invest in the best tech to manage your business operations, such as e-Commerce software, CRMs, accounting tools, project management systems, and more. You'll also need to stay on top of the latest trends in business technology and make sure that your software is always up-to-date to protect against cyber threats.

If you allow the benefits of using the technology around you to drive you, not only will you increase your productivity, but it will also ignite your passion for success in business.

Incorporate Self-Care Techniques Into Your Business Routine

Passion for success in business can also be enhanced by incorporating self-care techniques into your daily routine. After all, positive self-care habits can help you find balance and prevent burnout, so it's important to cultivate mindfulness in order to stay passionate and energized.

One of the best ways to stay motivated and passionate is to have a consistent daily routine that helps you stay organized. Dedicate time each day to taking care of yourself - that could be anything from doing yoga or going for a run, meditating, or simply taking some time to relax and reflect. That helps you re-calibrate your thoughts and give you a much-needed break from the hustle and bustle of running a business.

Also, the people around us can have a powerful effect on how we view ourselves and our goals, so make sure that your support network consists of positive individuals who inspire you. This could include mentors, colleagues, peers or even family members who understand the importance of self-care and are dedicated to helping you succeed. Additionally, networking with other like-minded individuals can spark creativity and give you new perspectives on how to approach business success.

By implementing these simple self-care tips into your daily life, you can create an environment where passion for success thrives easily.

Stay Motivated Even in the Face of Challenges

It's easy to get discouraged when you encounter obstacles with your business, but the most important thing is to stay motivated so that you can push through and continue to reach your goals!

Your environment can be a powerful tool in staying motivated and inspired - so don't be afraid to step outside of your comfort zone and try something new. That passion in you must find expression - it must not die!

Seek out learning opportunities in and around your community, such as workshops, seminars, or conferences. Here, you can find others in the same boat as you and gain insight on how they are dealing with challenges that you may be facing as well. Plus, industry leaders often give great talks and can offer valuable advice.

Having like-minded individuals who understand what challenges entrepreneurs face on a daily basis can be a great source of support. It can help you stay motivated! Find people who have similar interests and have succeeded in similar areas as yourself; this could include family and friends but also other business owners. Create conversations brainstorm ideas and troubleshoot potential challenges - the positive energy will help inspire you even more.

Make It Fun!

Make your environment fun. Take time away from work if needed so that you can come back refreshed with new ideas. Try out different activities, like going on hikes or exploring new places - find whatever sparks a flame inside of you that motivates your success.

Whether you're an entrepreneur, a freelancer, or a corporate executive, the key to long-term business success is finding and creating an environment that supports and encourages your goals. By optimizing your surroundings to reflect the things that you're passionate about and staying motivated to reach those ambitions, you'll be well on your way to realizing your true business potential.

Take a moment to recognize and analyze your environment, identify the areas that need improvement, and then take action to make the necessary changes. The journey to business success may be filled with obstacles, but by surrounding yourself with the right people, places and things, you can ignite the passion and determination needed to make it to the top.

The Impact of Business Ideology and Personal Opinions on Opportunities

Being too convinced of your business ideology or personal opinion that it cost you a chance of opportunity can become a mistake that can backfire in more ways than one. It's important to remember that in business, there is no one-size-fits-all solution. What works for one company may not be the right approach for another company. Your success depends on being flexible and open to new ideas.

But even when you think you've hit the sweet spot, your precious beliefs and opinions can still come back to haunt you if they aren't approached in the right way.

Whether intentional or not, the opinions and ideologies you express in a professional setting can have a huge impact on your chances of receiving an opportunity to do business. Poorly handling your opinions, or failing to account for someone else's point of view, can be the difference between gaining a deal and losing it.

Let me show you some of the consequences of sharing unchecked opinions. They can:

- alienate potential clients,
- discouraging potential partners from wanting to work with you,
- cause you to misunderstand customers' needs as there would be a disconnect between both parties,
- make you receive backlash from colleagues for failing to consider their positions, and
- impact the morale of team members due to unprofessional conduct.

It's best practice for any businessperson to always consider their position in relation to their partners, customers and team before making comments about matters of opinion. Doing so will help keep everyone aligned towards mutual success and build more meaningful relationships that can last long-term.

Understanding the Balance of Professionalism & Personal Opinion

It is important to remember that balance is strategic in expressing your business ideology and personal opinion. You need to find the delicate balance between showing your authenticity and displaying professionalism. It may be easy to express yourself in a way that makes you appear outspoken, but that same attitude could cost you an opportunity if it's too strong. It can be challenging to express, without ruffling feathers, that you are passionate about certain topics or disagree with others who may have opposing views.

The best approach is usually to remain level-headed and focus on solutions rather than getting caught up in conflicts. If you are feeling passionate about a certain topic, it is best to craft an articulate response that has substance and conveys your point professionally as opposed to making accusations or angrily stating your opinion. You never know who you might be working with in the future, so it's important to maintain a professional standard while also staying true to your beliefs.

Knowing Your Customer Is Essential to Business Success

You may have a strong business ideology or opinion of a particular matter - but when it comes to dealing with customers, you should be aware that your opinion and what they want are two very different things.

If you're trying to offer services or products to customers who don't follow your ideologies, you run the risk of potentially missing out on opportunities because of it. Consider this: customers want convenience and a good price for their product or service; if you hold yourself back from providing them with what they want, it's very likely that someone else will come in and provide them with those benefits instead.

Here are some tips to keep in mind when engaging customers, regardless of your own beliefs:

1. Be open-minded - try to focus on what the customer wants and needs rather than where you stand on certain matters.
2. Understand the market - while your opinions matter, they should not dictate how you treat potential clients or provide services/products. Learn more about the market to get an idea of the competition and customer needs.
3. Invest in research - do thorough research into the customer's industry and their own company objectives; this way, you'll have a better understanding of their needs and can tailor solutions accordingly.
4. Focus on providing solutions - rather than emphasizing your personal opinions, emphasize solutions that benefit both sides; this way, everyone is satisfied and no one feels like their side is being overlooked or ignored.

Being Flexible & Open-Minded Can Lead to More Opportunities

Sometimes the best way to land a business opportunity is by leaving your personal opinion and business ideology at the door. Flexibility and open-mindedness are essential for potential clients, because they can lead to more opportunities if you make sure to be flexible and willing to consider different solutions.

Being open-minded sets a positive tone in any business or personal relationship - it shows that you value their ideas and opinions, which can lead to more trust and collaboration. You might have your own thoughts about how something should be done, but being willing to hear out other options gives you a chance to really understand the client's needs.

Not only does being flexible make it easier for clients to trust you, it also broadens your horizons when considering different solutions. It's important not to judge something immediately but instead take a little time to think outside of the box. Doing so can open doors for new ideas that you wouldn't normally consider, which could provide the solution the client needs - and what a great feeling that is!

Being flexible and open-minded can give you an edge when vying for business opportunities, so don't be afraid to try something new.

Embracing a Growth Mindset Can Repair Mistakes & Open You Up to Better Prospects

What's key for business success? A growth mindset. Once you understand your mistakes and how to avoid them in the future, that's when the real benefit comes in - realizing all the possibilities open to you.

It's kind of like the 'bounce back' effect. When you accept that you can learn and grow from difficult experiences, then it's easier to:

1. Recognize how your opinion or beliefs may have become an obstacle in securing prospects
2. Adjust your frame of mind and focus on solutions
3. Become open to new solutions and opportunities

A growth mindset isn't just about repairing existing mistakes - it can open up entirely new possibilities for your business. By being committed to personal growth, learning from mistakes and embracing the change, it opens up a whole new array of customers, ideas or prospects. After all, any good relationship is built upon understanding and compromise. Allowing yourself to be more flexible with your opinions and perspectives can help you discover better opportunities down the line.

Managing the balance between your business ideology and personal opinion requires a delicate touch. Reveal only what is necessary in order to get the job done, and be self-aware about when it's best to keep quiet or maintain a professional distance. Doing so preserves your credibility, ensures respect from colleagues, and allows you to express yourself in an effective yet non-confrontational manner when the situation calls for it.

This kind of professionalism that nurtures creative expression can help ensure you maintain the opportunity of having a successful career in business. After all, who hasn't had a moment where their personal opinion has almost cost them a chance of opportunity? Being able to toe the line between professionalism and taking a stand on certain issues is key to your success in business.

At the end of the day, it's important to recognize the power of our words, and the potential they have to make or break our business opportunities. Our beliefs and ideas should be expressed in a respectful manner, without crossing the line into personal attacks. Before we voice our opinions and make statements, we should consider both the potential risks and opportunities associated with it.

Having an honest dialog and a respectful exchange of ideas is the way to build genuine relationships and trust, both of which are essential for business success. Ultimately, it's up to each of us to decide how to balance our personal opinions with our professional goals and keep our words from becoming liabilities.

Narrow-Minded belief: A Hindrance to business opportunity

Have you ever been presented with an exciting business opportunity only for it to be shot down by your team? From the outside looking in, it can be difficult to tell why. Team members may not have an adequate explanation, and you can't help but feel like they're missing out on something special.

The truth is that preconceived notions can be detrimental to the success of any business venture. These are the assumptions we make before we've taken the time to learn about a certain product or service, or understand how it could fit into our current strategies. Without taking that extra step to truly comprehend what's being presented, it's easy for narrow-minded assumptions to prevent progress and limit potential opportunities. How can you overcome these preconceived notions and maximize your business potential?

Understand that Traditional Business Models Can Limit Growth

You may find yourself being fooled by preconceived notions and traditional business models, which can limit the growth of your business. For example, have you ever been restricted from pursuing a certain opportunity because you assumed it was too costly to do so?

This is a common problem that can be avoided with a shift in mindset. With the right approaches, you can grow your business opportunities in ways that don't require large investments. For example, you could create a product or service for customers whose preferences are limited by their budget constraints or time constraints. You could also evaluate ways to outsource tasks and services that would otherwise have to be carried out internally.

When assessing potential business opportunities, it's important to think outside of the box and leave no stone unturned. Find creative solutions that respond to customer needs while driving maximum cost efficiency. This kind of approach requires an entrepreneurial mindset - one which shuns narrow-mindedness and embraces an innovative spirit instead.

Evaluate the Evidence for or Against a New Idea

When you're presented with an opportunity in business, it's important to take the time to evaluate it and consider whether or not it's a good fit. Often, our opinion of any given opportunity will be shaped by our experiences and preconceived notions we have about certain topics.

However, if you are really eager to get ahead in business, it is important to not let these beliefs stand in the way of a successful outcome. Before you discount the idea, take some time to do research and consider facts instead of relying on your intuition. Gather data that speaks for or against the proposal and create a comprehensive list of pros/cons so you can make an informed decision.

It may be easy to jump to conclusions based on your beliefs or experiences from the past, but make sure that these opinions are backed up by facts before dismissing them out of hand. Evaluate any evidence for or against an idea before making a final decision - it's the only way you can ensure that your business endeavors don't stumble because of narrow-mindedness.

Understand that New Ideas Can Solve Old Problems

It's easy to fall into the trap of believing something simply because everybody else does, but when it comes to business opportunities, narrow-minded beliefs can put an end to them before you've even had the chance to explore them.

The reality is that innovation and creativity can offer solutions to some of our oldest problems. After all, sometimes a brand new approach is the only way to get past an entrenched old one. So don't let preconceived notions and assumptions put an end to your business opportunities.

Yes, it's important to acknowledge and respect the traditional ways of doing things, but never be blinded by them. Just because something has been done a certain way for years doesn't mean that it can't be improved or done differently. Instead of viewing this as a challenge, embrace it as an opportunity for change and growth.

Also, instead of rejecting a new idea outright, consider what the potential implications could be if you gave it a try or implemented it in your company. Even if it doesn't work out in the long run, at least you've tried and learned something along the way - which could prove useful down the line.

Identify Areas For Improvement

While considering potential business opportunities, also identify areas in which existing solutions need improvement or change - then come up with creative ways of tackling these weaknesses. This approach could open up entire new markets that have yet to be tapped into by your competition.

The Art of Risk Assessment: Knowing When to Take the Leap

Risk assessment is an essential tool in any business. Sometimes, taking a risk can be the difference between success and failure. However, it's important to remember that not all risks are created equal and some of them can be avoided with the right kind of analysis.

One important thing to keep in mind in risk assessment is that sometimes we can get too caught up in our own narrow-minded beliefs. We may prefer to stay within our comfort zone and reject opportunities that could potentially lead to great things.

In order to free ourselves from this kind of rigidity, we must start by questioning our assumptions about what is possible for us and for our business. This means examining our biases and preconceived notions about a particular situation or opportunity before jumping into action. It also means seeking out different perspectives from people who are knowledgeable or experienced in the area you're looking into.

Evaluate Pros and Cons

Once you have a better understanding of what's out there, make sure you evaluate both the pros and cons of any potential risks - both financially and emotionally. Consider all the possible outcomes so that when you make your decision, you're making it from a place of knowledge rather than simply shooting from the hip.

By taking the time to do your due diligence on any potential business opportunity, you can make sure that you don't miss out on something amazing because of your own narrow-mindedness or lack of knowledge.

Don't let preconceived notions put an end to a business opportunity before you've even given it a chance. It's easy to hear something and jump to conclusions without understanding the full context or doing your own research. That's why it's vital to keep an open mind and view other people's opinions as just that - opinions.

What happens too often is that we form our own opinion based on what we think we know, but in reality, what you think you know might be completely wrong. It can be hard not to fall into this trap, but if you want to get the most out of business opportunities, then it pays to stay objective and take the time to do your own research instead of relying on hearsay.

Research

Doing ample research will help you understand the situation better and avoid being misguided by false assumptions. When looking into potential business opportunities, take the time to research: the market industry, company culture, potential competitors, the product or service potential clients are looking for, and any legal implications that may need addressing.

Research is needed in exploring new business opportunities, for both entrepreneurs and employees alike. If you want to really get the most out of them and take advantage of them, then don't let preconceived notions stop you from seizing the moment.

Harness Creativity and Innovation

Don't let preconceived notions put an end to potential creativity and innovation. You might have a great idea, but it could be shut down with a simple "that won't work" from someone who is stuck in an old way of thinking. It's important to find ways to harness your creative juices and use them to drive success.

Here are a few ways you can do that:

1. Listen more than you talk. When brainstorming, make sure everyone has the space and chance to share their ideas - you may be surprised at what comes to the surface.
2. Ensure everyone feels heard and supported – encourage diverse voices and viewpoints in order to bring out differing perspectives on how best to tackle a problem or issue.
3. Try something new every once in a while - not only will it encourage creative thinking, but it also helps develop an agile mindset which can be of great importance when launching new products or services.
4. Don't forget that failure is part of the process - it can often lead to unexpected success if you're willing to learn from the mistakes and use them for future improvements or solutions!

By allowing creativity and innovation into your business opportunities, you set yourself up for greater success in the long run. So don't let anyone limit your potential just because they don't think outside the box - take risks and watch your idea blossom into something even better than you expected.

If you let narrow-minded beliefs or preconceived notions stand in your way, you'll miss out on valuable business opportunities. It's up to us to open our minds and look at things from a different perspective. By doing so, we can be open to new ideas, people, or products and have a better understanding of the business opportunities that exist. Not only that, but we can be more creative and innovative when it comes to problem solving.

Be willing to step out of your comfort zone and take risks, and don't be afraid of failure - because it's in taking those risks that you'll grow and develop. When you take the time to understand a situation in a different way, you can break through walls that were formerly impassable. Don't let preconceived notions put an end to your business opportunities - broaden your outlook and be open to possibilities.

Chapter 2

Not Today, I Will do it Tomorrow

Lack of Passion Gives Birth to Procrastination

It's very possible that you find yourself struggling to stick to a project, deadline, or set of goals. One minute you're filled with enthusiasm, and the next your motivation has waned, and instead of moving forward toward what matters most to you, you find yourself procrastinating.

It's not always easy to pinpoint the source of this resistance - but it turns out that lack of passion can often be a major factor in why we procrastinate. Passion is an engine that fuels us to take action, but when it's missing? That's when procrastination starts to set in.

This chapter will explore how a distinct lack of passion can lead to procrastination - and what you can do about it. Whether you're feeling less than inspired by a project or need motivation for getting things done in general, I will provide some useful insights and tips for reclaiming your mojo and boosting productivity. Let's dive in!

How Can Lack of Passion Lead to Procrastination?

When you lack passion for something, it's often hard to stay motivated to do the project. You don't feel the same spark of enthusiasm or desire to take action. As a result, you can find yourself constantly procrastinating on completing it.

The longer you wait, the bigger a hurdle it becomes to start working on it again, and the more effort and motivation is required to finish. Eventually, procrastination itself can become an unintended consequence of lacking passion - a cycle that's difficult to break out of.

You can avoid this spiral by taking deliberate action as soon as possible. Doing so will help you stay focused and energized in order to complete the task at hand. For example, if you know a project will challenge your knowledge and skillset, set small goals that break down into achievable chunks and reward yourself for progress made along the way. That makes the task much less daunting and help keep your focus until completion.

Now, why are you lacking in passion and constantly procrastinating on projects?

Lack of Excitement

When eagerness and curiosity are lacking, enthusiasm is rarely felt. If you don't feel excited about your project or task at hand, chances are you won't feel much passion for it, either. Lacking excitement can make it difficult to find motivation, which can lead to procrastination down the line.

Incorrect Prioritization

When there is too much on your plate and not enough focus on the tasks that bring you joy or satisfaction, it can zap away at what little passion you have for the project. If you find yourself allocating your time for tasks that aren't necessary or impactful, this can further reduce your enthusiasm and result in more procrastination.

Fixed Mindset

A fixed mindset can also take its toll on your passion levels - if you think that you're unable to reach a goal or learn something new, this can make it harder for you to stay passionate about the project and make any meaningful progress towards completing it. Even if failure is inevitable, having an open mindset is relevant to staying engaged in the process.

By taking steps to address any of these issues, such as refocusing priorities or shifting your perspective towards having an open mindset, you might find that your passion levels will increase - along with your ability to stay focused and motivated on each project.

The Emotional and Psychological Effects of a Lack of Passion

If you ever find yourself stuck in a vicious cycle of procrastination in your work, it could be that the problem is less about lacking motivation, and more about lacking passion. When you lack passion and enthusiasm for a task, it can have a huge impact on your cognitive functions, and cause you to become demotivated. This makes it incredibly difficult to focus on your work, since it takes more effort to muster up the energy to do the task. What then are the expected impacts?

Emotional Impact

When you lack passion, emotion can play a huge role in how motivated you are to complete the task. Without that enthusiasm or excitement for what you're doing, it's incredibly easy to get overwhelmed by the task, leading to depression and frustration.

Cognitive Impact

Not having enthusiasm for a given project can also lead to cognitive issues such as poor concentration skills and memory difficulties. This can cause procrastination from fear of not being able to adequately do the job. Additionally, people with limited amounts of passion can struggle with making decisions, as they are unable to generate any motivation from within themselves.

Without finding a way reignite some passion for the task at hand, people may find themselves constantly struggling with procrastination and failing again and again.

How Do You Get out of This Mess?

Get Excited About What You're Doing

When there's no passion, you may have lost sight of why you're doing the project in the first place. Try to find something about it that excites you - whether it's a potential outcome or rewards system - that will help energize your effort.

Remind Yourself of Your Purpose

It's possible that your passion for what you're working on is buried under mundane tasks and mundane process. Take a moment to remind yourself why this task matters - tapping into your "why" often helps generate more enthusiasm for tackling challenging tasks.

Break It Down Into Smaller Tasks

If the overall task feels too daunting, break it down into smaller chunks that are more manageable. It takes away some of the pressure of trying to do everything all at once - enabling you to focus on doing one thing at a time, as opposed to all of them at once.

Reconnecting with passion can be hard when all of your energy goes into procrastination mode, but with a little patience and self-reflection, you can keep working toward an end goal while enjoying the journey at the same time.

Reflect and Identify Your Goals

Take some time to reflect on why you started this project in the first place and write down specific goals you want to accomplish. Once you have identified your goals, break them down into actionable steps so they won't seem so daunting.

Prioritize Tasks

Think about which tasks are most important and should be done first, then start working on those. Having an organized plan can help you stay motivated and focused while ensuring that the most critical tasks are done first.

Make Good Use of Your Time

Rather than aimlessly scrolling through social media or watching TV all day, create a schedule that allows for breaks from work and free time for yourself. That will help to ensure that you make the best use of your time and also motivate yourself when needed. Additionally, setting realistic deadlines for each task helps keep procrastination at bay as it gives you something tangible to work towards.

Never also underestimate the power of positive affirmations and rewards! When tackling difficult tasks or feeling unmotivated, take some time to remind yourself why this project is important to you or reward yourself with a treat once a task is completed – it can be just what you need to get out of your funk.

It's easy to fall into the trap of procrastination when you don't have enough passion for a project. You may start the project with enthusiasm, only to have it quickly fizzle out when the task becomes too difficult or time-consuming.

But the good news is that you can overcome the lack of passion and procrastination pattern. It's important to recognize the signs that point to a lack of passion and reframe your thoughts to remember why you're doing something and to stay motivated. Also, try breaking the task down into smaller, more achievable chunks, and focus on the rewards that come from completing the task.

Having passion for a project can make a world of difference to how motivated you are to actually see it through. Taking the time to find the passion and focus may be just the thing that helps you beat procrastination.

A Change of Environment Can Help You Focus

The truth is, productivity is rarely about our capabilities - it's more often about the environment we're working in. That's why creating an environment that is conducive to productivity is so important if you want to maximize your efforts and make progress towards your goals.

If you are feeling unproductive, it might be time to make a change in your environment. It's been proven that changes to our environment can have a positive impact on our productivity.

Here are some of the advantages of creating an environment to maximize productivity:

Increased Focus

Changing your environment can help you focus on tasks and complete them more efficiently. Without distractions, like a TV or people talking, it's easier to stay on track and complete projects faster.

Improved Concentration

By eliminating anything that might be distracting, you'll be able to prioritize tasks and maintain concentration for longer periods of time. The right environment will also help you achieve better results in less time and with fewer distractions.

A Motivated Mindset

When we feel motivated and inspired, it's easier to stay focused and productive instead of feeling overwhelmed or stuck. The right environment can create this sense of motivation and give us the boost we need to tackle projects without getting sidetracked or discouraged.

Take some time to evaluate your current workspace and see if you can make any changes that will help increase your productivity!

Do you know the environment that you're working in can make it difficult for you to focus on work or a big project? It's important to analyze your current workspace, which can give insight into how productive you are and where you might need improvement. Think about elements like: what sounds do you hear when working? Are there any natural light sources available? How easy is it for you to take breaks when needed? Is your workspace comfortable?

These effects on your environment can either help or hinder your productivity. If noise is a distraction, consider finding a quieter space. If natural light helps boost productivity, try rearranging furniture and setting up your desk near a window if possible. Adjusting the temperature of the room and adding comfortable furniture can also make it easier to stay focused for longer periods of time.

By taking the time to analyze how your workspace affects productivity, you'll be able to make the changes needed for success and reach your goals faster.

You can also try these:

1. **De-clutter:** Make sure your desk is tidy and all of your items are stored in an orderly fashion. It helps you concentrate better without having to shift through stacks of papers or rummage through drawers for items you need for a task.
2. **Adjust the lighting:** You need just the right amount of natural light and a lamp with an adjustable brightness setting. Too much light can cause strain on your eyes, while too little light can hinder concentration.
3. **Introduce some plants:** Adding plants to your workspace are not only esthetically pleasing, but they also help improve the air quality, which in turn helps improve concentration and productivity levels.
4. **Keep it clean:** Having a clean and organized space makes it easier to focus on tasks at hand,

as there's less chance of getting distracted by unorganized clutter or dirt around you.

Getting rid of distractions is also essential to concentrating and achieving your goals. What techniques are perfect for such a situation?

Change your environment

Choose a place that is comfortable to work and free from potential distractions. If this isn't possible, consider ways in which you can make the environment more conducive to concentration - for example, playing music or using earplugs to drown out external noise.

Go for breaks

Take regular breaks throughout the day in order to help you concentrate better. Take time for yourself - go for a walk, have a snack or chat with a colleague. This will give you time to reset and will help reduce fatigue and stress too!

Use technology

Many modern devices have features designed to help minimize distractions. For instance, iPhones have DND mode which silences incoming notifications; Windows 10 has the Focus Assist feature which allows users to selectively disable notifications; and many laptops now come with 'concentration' settings that reduce brightness, blue light levels and other elements of the UI that could distract users from their tasks at hand.

By changing your environment, taking regular breaks and utilizing available technology, you will be able to focus on your tasks better and maximize productivity.

Add Color and Decor

We all know that having a colorful and esthetic environment can bring life and energy to any space. And it turns out that adding color and decor to your workspace can help you stay motivated and maximize productivity even more.

In fact, one survey found that 40% of respondents said paintings, photographs or artwork in an office improved their ability to stay focused on work tasks. And participants said that these decorations help create a positive atmosphere where creative ideas could be generated.

So to spruce up your workspace:

- Think about how some simple changes can make a big impact on your productivity and drive to achieve your goals:
- Include shades of blue or green in the room - doctors have long theorized these hues help provide a calming affect
- Incorporate natural light into the room - studies suggest natural lighting helps reduce depression, fatigue and eyestrain
- Choose items with character - choose furniture pieces that reflect your personality or bring a sense of comfort like bean bags or festive rugs
- Decorate with subtle reminders of goals - use prints or quotes as visual reminders of your ambitions or aspirations
- Make sure you're comfortable - there's nothing worse than an uncomfortable chair when you're trying to focus on tasks at hand.

When your desk is full of unnecessary items, it's hard to concentrate. Keep only the essentials on your desk: laptop, mouse, phone, and anything else that might help with productivity. Put away all other items - books, folders, coffee cups - so that your workspace is distraction-free.

Invest in Good Lighting

Lighting is necessary for productivity - if it's too bright or too dark, you'll struggle to focus on work. Invest in an adjustable lamp with adjustable brightness settings so that you can create the perfect lighting level for yourself.

Add Some Greenery

Bringing a bit of nature into your workspace can have calming effects and help boost creativity and productivity. Try adding some plants - real or faux - to create a more uplifting environment.

Changing your environment and optimizing it for productivity can be a great way to get more out of your day. Whether it's removing distractions from your workspace or creating a more inviting workspace, optimizing your environment can help you stay focused and motivated towards achieving your goals.

It's important to be mindful of the environment you're working in when trying to maximize productivity. Everyone is different and our surroundings can have a huge effect on how we think, act, and perform. Whether it's taking regular breaks, listening to music, or changing your work space, give yourself the best chance of success by creating a stimulating yet calming environment.

Utilizing Rewards to Achieve Goals

Instead of forcing yourself to do a task, why not motivate yourself with rewards? Making tangible goals with rewards can help take the drudgery out of chores and inspire you to achieve them. It can be as simple as giving yourself a reward after you finish something. Small tokens like your favorite sweet treat or an hour of uninterrupted Netflix time can go a long way in keeping you motivated. But the key is finding something that incentivizes you and your work – something that creates value for you instead of being a burden.

In its simplest form, a reward is something that motivates people to do something: a target you set for yourself, or a task someone else asks of you. You can think of it as a prize for completing your job. Rewards come in all shapes and sizes - sometimes they're physical (like money), and other times they're mental (like the sense of accomplishment).

Rewards can also provide incentive to complete tasks faster by increasing challenge and difficulty levels. For example, if you ask yourself to complete a task within a certain timeframe, chances are you won't be motivated unless there's a reward involved. By offering rewards, you create an even greater incentive to complete the task on time.

Rewards can even be action-oriented - say, for example, taking the weekend off if you finish all your tasks by Friday evening. The possibilities are virtually limitless; all it takes is some creativity and motivation to choose the right rewards that will inspire you or someone else to reach their targets.

In setting yourself up for success, rewards can be a powerful motivator. But which type of reward is right for the task at hand? Let me break down the two types of rewards you can use to get motivated and accomplish your goals.

1. **Positive Reinforcement** rewards provide an immediate reward after a goal or task is completed. This can include things like financial bonuses, words of praise or recognition, or intangible rewards like extra time off. Positive reinforcement is great for tasks that may require an initial burst of motivation and follow-through.
2. **Delayed Gratification** rewards are given only after completing a more challenging and longer task. These types of rewards could be tangible items like gift cards, or experiences such as a weekend away or movie night with friends. Delayed gratification helps build momentum with tasks that need sustained effort over time.

Whether employing positive reinforcement or delayed gratification, finding the right reward for the job can help you stay on track and reach your goals faster!

What Are the Benefits of Implementing Rewards?

Rewards help focus our attention on what we need to do and they bring a meaningful purpose to the task at hand. But there's more to rewards than just that! Here are some of the benefits of implementing rewards:

Motivation

Rewards can have a powerful psychological effect on us. They give us something tangible and concrete that we can strive for; they create an incentive that makes us work harder so we can collect the reward. This phenomenon is known as the "carrot and stick" approach - visualizing the reward ahead will drive people to work harder in order to get it.

Positive Reinforcement

Rewards are also great for positive reinforcement. Rewarding someone for their hard work encourages them to continue their effort, as well as gives them confidence in their capabilities. The feeling of accomplishment will motivate them to keep going and strive for better results in the future.

Focusing & Habits Formation

Rewards can also help us focus on what needs to be done and form habits around completing tasks. By linking rewards with specific activities, you create an automatic response that helps you focus on what needs to be done while avoiding distractions or procrastination. It also helps build good habits such as staying organized or creating schedules ahead of time so that tasks can be completed efficiently.

How to Set Up Effective Reward Systems

What you want to think of at this stage is: "How do I set up an effective reward system?"

Define Your Goals

The first step when putting together any rewards system is to define your goals. Sit down and think about what you want to achieve. What tasks do you want to complete? Be realistic - don't try and take on too much at once. It will only lead to overwhelm and disappointment. All you need is to set specific, easy-to-understand goals. Decide what you want to achieve and create a plan with step-by-step tasks. It ensures you stay focused on your goal and make it more achievable in the long run.

Set Those Rewards

The next step is to set rewards for each goal you want to achieve. Making the rewards motivating enough, without being too extravagant, encourages positive behavior in the long-term. Rewards can come in many forms: a new gadget, a night out, or even the feeling of satisfaction that comes with completing a task.

Once you have your plan in place, create a reward system for yourself. This can be anything from treats, like a night out with friends or watching a movie, to tangible rewards like purchasing something for yourself. The important thing is that it must be something that excites and motivates you when you're feeling stuck.

Keep Track of Progress

Keep track of your progress as you work towards your goal so that you can give yourself a reward when it's earned. Once you've started your reward system, make sure to track progress and stick with it. Research shows that simply writing down your progress helps increase focus on the task at hand and raises motivation levels across the board. You can also use tracking apps or other technology to help keep track of your tasks and ensure that each goal is met. By setting clear goals and tracking progress, you'll be able to reach your goals faster than ever before.

Make sure you break up the rewards into smaller chunks so that the overall task doesn't seem overwhelming and so that there are milestones along the way that can help sustain motivation.

By celebrating your successes and rewarding yourself for hard work, not only will it give you motivation to complete the task at hand but also inspire optimism that future tasks can be accomplished too - because all those rewards will add up.

What should you avoid?

Things might not always go according to plan though, so you should also remember to avoid some common pitfalls when setting up reward systems for yourself.

Don't Use Incentives for Everything

It might be tempting to use incentives for every task and goal you have, but this can actually backfire as it can condition people to expect a reward whenever they do something. Rewards should be something your look forward to, not just something you expect as a matter of course.

Don't Overdo It

It's important not to overdo reward systems, or they might end up becoming less effective in motivating people to do tasks or complete goals. While it's great to reward yourself for completing tasks, be mindful of how often you're doing it; too much and it's easy to become less motivated.

Avoid Negative Consequences

Negative consequences are an ineffective way of motivating people; rather than making them more likely to complete tasks, it could make them disheartened and demoralized. Instead, focus on the positive rewards that come with completing tasks - the sense of accomplishment and satisfaction can be a great motivator!

So, rewards are a great way to add an extra incentive to achieving the tasks you set for yourself, and they provide an effective way to stay motivated in the long run. Rewards are individualized, so it's important to find an incentive that works for you. Whether it's a piece of candy, a film night, or a weekend away, having something to look forward to can help you focus and power through to the end. And, if you can't seem to stay motivated, try breaking your tasks down into small, achievable goals and reward yourself for each step.

Rewards are a powerful tool to get motivated, so don't be afraid to take advantage of them! It may take some trial and error, but once you find the reward system that works for you, you'll be on your way to achieving your goals.

Using Progress Notes to Monitor Personal tasks

You're a busy bee, juggling many tasks and multiple interests. You know you're making progress, but how can you tell for sure? It's always frustrating when you think you're making strides in the right direction, only to realize that those strides were mostly in circles.

You need a way to track your progress across all the projects you have going on. Enter progress notes - your tool for staying organized and on-track with each of your goals. But there's more to it than just writing down what you did yesterday; there's an art to using progress notes effectively.

Progress notes are a great way to keep track of personal tasks, habits, and goals. They provide an easy, yet effective way to measure your own progress and hold yourself accountable. But what exactly are they?

Put simply, progress notes are short, written summaries of your progress towards personal objectives. They usually include things like goals you've set, any changes that have been made in the pursuit of those goals, and any obstacles or successes you've experienced in reaching them. In some cases, progress note lengths can vary - from one sentence to several paragraphs - depending on the type of work being done.

If you're looking for a way to stay motivated and ensure that your hard work is paying off over time, then progress notes may be the answer for you. Not only do they help make sure that you're making headway on your projects and goals in a systematic way, but they can also help you develop better goal setting strategies for next time around!

Why Create Progress Notes?

Creating progress notes is a simple way to document your work journey, track successes and failures, and ensure that you stay on task.

Progress notes help you stay organized and accountable to yourself for the tasks you plan to complete each day or week. With progress notes, you can conveniently keep a written record of all of your goals, areas of focus and approaches used to achieve them. Writing regular progress notes can also help you reflect on your performance and set measurable targets for future tasks.

Progress notes help you to:

- **Track Long-term Goals**: Regularly writing down your goals in a structured way allows you to easily monitor your long-term objectives.
- **Identify Trends**: Progress notes let you consistently record your successes and failures over time so that you can identify any trends in your performance or workflow.
- **Stay Motivated**: Seeing evidence of progress - even small successes - can help keep you motivated to reach larger goals.

What Should Be Included in Progress Notes?

Now that you know why you need to take progress notes, let us figure out what should be included.

Things to Note

Things like goals, tasks, sub-tasks, progress evaluation (e.g., is it going as planned?), deadlines (have they been met?) and results should all be included and tracked in your progress notes. This way, you'll have a clear overview of where you stand in terms of accomplishing your goals.

Making Adjustments In Real Time

Another thing that should be mentioned in your progress notes is whether any changes have been made. Are there any adjustments to working hours or project deadlines? These are just a few questions that should be answered so that you can make any necessary updates on the fly. Plus, if there's anything significant that has changed since the last time you looked at your progress notes, then it's important to record these details from now on - so there's no confusion later on down the line.

Progress notes are an effective way to monitor how well you're doing on personal tasks or projects. As long as your progress notes include the right information and data points (goals, tasks, sub-tasks, etc.), then it should help keep you informed and organized. And remember: By making adjustments in real time - based on what's written down - you can stay focused and motivated as well.

Now, how exactly do you use these?

First Note Down All Your Progress

It can be easy to forget about something that's been done already, especially when you're engrossed in the task itself. The best way around this is to actually record all of your progress as it happens, so when you come back to the task later, everything is documented and ready for review.

Establish Milestones and Goals

When working on a project, it's important to set milestones and goals that will help break down your work into manageable chunks and spur frequent wins. Progress notes are perfect for this - they let you track these chunks easily and clearly so that it's easy to identify which parts have been completed, which ones require more attention or could still be improved on.

Be Flexible with Adjustments

Projects rarely go as planned from start to finish - there are always adjustments that need to be made throughout the process. Having progress notes makes it easier for you to look back at what's been done and adjust as needed without losing too much time or having duplicate work being done.

By utilizing progress notes correctly, monitoring personal tasks is more efficient than ever before. So if your goal is set up a system for success - and get things done - progress notes can be an invaluable tool in your arsenal.

We have established that progress notes are a great tool to help you keep track of your progress and stay on top of your tasks. From setting goals and tracking deadlines to getting feedback from yourself, progress notes can help you stay on the path to success.

The bottom line is to find the progress notes system that works best for you. You don't want to get overwhelmed or bogged down in the details, so it's important that you use a system that works for you and makes monitoring your tasks and making progress simpler, not more complex.

No matter which system you choose, the most important thing is to make sure that you're using progress notes in order to take action and keep moving forward. So, get started and make sure you're making progress!

CHAPTER 3

Confidence Is the Base for All Your Outcomings

Doing Just What You Already Love Boosts Confidence

Everyone has moments when they feel a little down or lacking in confidence. As much as we try to tell ourselves that we're worth it, sometimes it's hard to believe. But don't worry – there's something you can do about it.

You know those activities that you love doing? Whether it's playing video games, painting, running, writing, or anything else, indulging in those things can help you get back your confidence and make you feel good again. Doing the things you like can help bring out the best in you, and give your self-esteem a boost.

It might seem counter-intuitive to do something just for fun when you're feeling blue, but it helps.

This chapter will explore how taking part in activities that make us happy can also make us more confident over time.

What Does It Mean to Do What You Like?

Doing what you like - or, said another way, pursuing your passions - doesn't have to mean achieving a certain level of mastery or becoming an expert. What matters is to find something that excites you and just go for it.

Maybe you love painting but haven't touched a brush yet. Or perhaps you've been meaning to try out a new hobby, like yoga or tap dancing. Doing something that captures your attention, encourages creativity and brings joy will not only help boost your confidence, but also bring a new purpose into your life that you may never have realized before.

It could be something simple, like reading every day or taking up photography as a hobby. Or, maybe it's something more adventurous and daring - that's okay too! Whatever it is, challenge yourself to step outside of your comfort zone - because when we do the things we love and keep learning new skills along the way, we are given the opportunity to be the best version of ourselves.

Understanding the Benefits of Doing What You Like

One of the best ways to boost your confidence is to do something you really enjoy. Doing activities, you like can help you relax, increase your self-esteem and remind you of what a great person you are.

Benefits of doing what you like include:

- **Feeling more confident:** Doing something that makes you happy helps fill your cup with happiness and courage. It can often give your mood a much needed lift, especially when feeling down or overwhelmed.
- **Increased positive self-talk:** Taking time to do things that lighten your spirits will help combat any negative thoughts or worries. This can in turn lead to increased positive self-talk and less anxiety in the long run.
- **Developing better relationships:** Doing activities that bring joy can also help strengthen existing relationships, as well as build new ones. By engaging in activities with someone else, it gives a chance for people to connect on an emotional level and share experiences together.

Doing what brings you joy is necessary for not only boosting confidence, but for overall mental wellbeing too. Taking time out of the day - no matter what it is - will help boost your energy levels, make you feel content and give yourself a sense of purpose.

When you do the things you like, you're going to feel good and your confidence will skyrocket. Not only that, but doing something that brings you joy or satisfaction will give you a sense of accomplishment, which can be a great motivator for pushing yourself to do more.

When you do something that makes you feel proud of yourself, it's like a pat on the back from your own personal cheer-leading squad. It demonstrates to yourself that you can accomplish things and reach goals, even if they may not seem too important to other people. This in turn makes it easier for you to tackle bigger tasks, as well as helping build up your self-esteem in general.

Getting into a productive mindset and tackling tasks with enthusiasm gives us a sense of accomplishment and allows us to feel proud at the end of the day no matter how small the task was. This is especially true when we work on things we enjoy because it allows us to stay focused and get more done without getting bored or restless. Feeling productive encourages us do more and be more confident in our decisions and abilities.

Doing things that make you happy gives you an outlet for stress relief and helps remind us of why we were passionate about something in the first place. Whether it's playing an instrument, painting or anything else, enjoying activities is great for our mental wellbeing because it boosts our confidence in ourselves, both professionally and personally.

Identifying Your Preferences and Interests

It is very important to figure out what you like and what your preferences and interests are. There are many ways to do this. You could take some time to reflect on your experiences, including places you've traveled, books you've read, or classes you've taken. You might also look into activities that have been tried and tested by others that have similar interests.

A great way to start is by taking inventory of your past successes - what have been the most rewarding experiences for you? What activities did you enjoy the most? Make a list of all the things that you liked doing and then try to narrow them down and focus on one or two areas. That will give you a good jumping-off point for finding opportunities to explore your interests further and practice them in a safe environment before showing them off to the world.

From there, all that's left is to find ways of incorporating these activities into your life in new and creative ways. The more time and energy you put into doing things that make you feel good and confident, the happier and more fulfilled life will be.

How Do You Handle Self-Doubt While Doing What You Love?

Doing activities, you like can give you a huge confidence boost. But, that doesn't mean there won't be moments of self-doubt. After all, the more you do something, the harder it can get to stay motivated and keep going.

So Recognize Imposter Syndrome

Sometimes it may feel like you're an imposter - like someone else is better than you at this particular activity. That's called Imposter Syndrome and it's fairly common. The best way to handle self-doubt when engaging in activities that make you feel good is to recognize that feeling for what it is - Imposter Syndrome - and acknowledge it for what it is: an emotion that will pass.

Build Yourself Up with Positive Affirmations

Another great way to handle self-doubt when doing activities that make you feel good is to remind yourself why they are important to you and why they make you feel good. Positive affirmations can really help with this because they build your confidence in yourself. For example, instead of saying "I will never be able to do this" try saying "I am capable of mastering this skill if I work hard and practice regularly" or "I am excited about my progress so far and I look forward to getting better at every day."

By recognizing your feelings of self-doubt for what they are, building yourself up with positive affirmations, setting realistic expectations for yourself, and focusing on practice rather than perfection you can learn how to handle those moments of self-doubt and keep doing the things that make you feel good.

Another secret to building the needed confidence to succeed is to create time for that thing you love - create time for yourself. It can have a positive impact on your confidence.

Doing activities that we enjoy – whether it's going to the beach, playing video games with friends, reading a book, or baking something delicious – gives us an opportunity to focus on ourselves and appreciate the little moments of joy. It helps us stay in touch with our identity and helps build our self-esteem.

Plus, being able to connect with yourself and enjoy moments of peace is one of the most important reasons why it's essential to make room for doing what you love.

Let me share some tips on how you can make time for doing what you love.

- Make a list of activities that bring you joy and prioritize them over other commitments.
- Set aside at least an hour per week or two hours per month for an activity or hobby you enjoy.
- Work these activities into your routine so that they become habits.
- Don't feel guilty about planting your feet firmly in something that you enjoy.
- Take advantage of opportunities to share your passions with others.

By making time for doing what you love, you're able to de-stress and take a break from reality - which can be quite powerful for building confidence and improving your mood.

To sum up, doing the things you love can be a great way to boost your confidence, feel good, and also make meaningful connections with those around you. Learning more about yourself, understanding what activities make you feel content and full of life - and then making time for them - can make all the difference.

When it comes to confidence and wellbeing, the best thing you can do is to strive to be the best version of yourself. Be proud of the unique qualities that you bring to the table, of the progress you have made, and of the people in life who have helped you along the way. It's okay to make mistakes and to falter, because being authentic is the greatest superpower of all.

Confident People Are Always Going to Succeed in Business

Intelligence, ambition, and hard work play a role, but it's confidence that really sets them apart. It's like they have a secret weapon. They take advantage of opportunities, speak their mind, and create networks with ease. So why is it that confident people always seem to get ahead in business? To find out more about this phenomenon, let's take an insightful look at why confident people excel in business.

It's more than just having the right attitude; there are deeper psychological and sociological forces at play here.

I will talk to you about those forces – from social proof to self-efficacy – and how you can harness them for your own success.

What Does It Mean to Be Confident?

Confidence is a crucial element for achieving success in business. But what does it actually mean to be confident? It's more than just having a great attitude and believing in yourself - it's about having the self-assurance to take risks, trust your intuition, and build strong relationships with your team. Confident people understand the value of failure. They don't shy away from setbacks; instead, they are brave enough to recognize the opportunities that arise from mistakes. They are willing to try new things and adapt their strategies when necessary. They use their experience to gain valuable insights and stay ahead of their competition.

Confident people also have an unwavering sense of themselves and their capabilities. They know exactly what they bring to the table, which gives them the power to make decisions that are informed by past successes and missteps. This self-awareness allows them to confidently navigate situations without fear or hesitation, resulting in better outcomes for all involved.

At the heart of a confident person is resilience. No matter how difficult a situation may be, they remain calm, work hard, and maintain positive energy throughout the process. This steady drive for excellence results in improved performance, even under pressure or challenging circumstances.

Confidence is an essential trait for success in business. It enables you to take risks, make decisions quickly, and stand up for yourself. In fact, many studies suggest that confidence plays a crucial role in achieving business success. Confident people tend to be more persuasive. They are more likely to express their thoughts and opinions clearly, which can make them stand out from the competition. Additionally, they have higher emotional intelligence - meaning they can better understand and manage both their own emotions and those of others. This ability helps them build relationships more easily and establish trust in difficult business situations.

Confident people are not afraid of failure - they view failure as an opportunity to learn and improve rather than letting it bring them down. They also understand that failure is part of the process of achieving success; they will keep trying until they find a successful solution instead of giving up after the first few attempts. This resilience is one of the main characteristics that sets them apart from less confident people in the business world.

Benefits of an Increased Sense of Self-Confidence

Being confident brings a lot of benefits in being successful in business. It gives you the self-assurance to take risks and make decisions without feeling like you are going to fail. With that courage, comes an increase in the odds of success.

What's more, when your confidence increases, your performance improves too. That is because our minds are powerful things - and when we feel strong about what we are doing, our bodies respond better and we get more out of it. So what are the gains?

Growth Opportunities

The confidence to go after what you want can be a huge asset in the business world. People with confidence often have higher work ethics, which can help them stand out from among their peers and give them new opportunities for growth.

A Positive Attitude

Confident people also possess a "can do" attitude which helps them tackle difficult tasks with enthusiasm and drive. This positive outlook gives them a unique perspective on problems that allows them to come up with creative solutions.

Inspire Others

People who exude self-assurance project positive energy around them which helps uplift their co-workers and build healthy relationships in the workplace. This creates an inspirational environment where everyone is encouraged to excel and grow together towards success.

Strengthening Your Resilience to Overcome Challenges

Confident people don't shy away from challenges - they face them head on. This is why confident people tend to do better in business. They are not afraid to take risks, even when the stakes are high, which gives them an advantage that less confident people don't have.

This resilience strengthens over time and with practice, making confident people even better at overcoming challenges they may encounter in their business endeavors. For example, consider a confident business leader who faces a tough decision - they may take a risk by doing something unconventional and it could turn out to be an amazing success. On the other hand, if it doesn't work out, they won't give up - they will continue to try new approaches until they find the best one.

Confidence also gives you the courage to admit when you are wrong and adjust your strategies accordingly. When faced with a complex problem, rather than shying away from it, confident people will relentlessly search for creative solutions that can help them overcome any obstacle in their way. With this kind of confidence-fueled resilience, many business leaders have gone on to achieve great success.

Keys to Developing a Greater Sense of Self-Confidence

Having a greater sense of self-confidence is key to succeeding in the business world. The good news is that it's possible to develop this trait and use it to your advantage if you are willing to put in a little work.

Here are some of the keys to developing a greater sense of self-confidence:

Acknowledging Your Good Qualities

It's important to take time to recognize and acknowledge your natural abilities and special talents. Whether you excel in problem solving, creative thinking, communication or any other business-related skills, taking note of them can remind you why you are well-suited for success.

Knowing Your Weaknesses

No one is perfect and it's just as important to learn about your weaknesses as it is your strengths. Understanding what areas need improvement can help you make adjustments and improvements that will increase your overall confidence.

Establishing Goals

Having goals gives life purpose, structure and focus. Setting achievable goals helps create feelings of accomplishment which can boost confidence levels.

Celebrating Achievements

Take time to recognize even the small successes along the way by rewarding yourself with something meaningful like a day off or new lunch spot when you reach particular milestones on your way to achieving your goals.

Common Mistakes Made by Unconfident People in Business

No matter how hard someone works, if they don't have confidence in their abilities, there's a good chance they won't be successful in business. You can avoid the common mistakes made by unconfident people that tend to hold them back.

Not Taking Risks

The biggest mistake that unconfident people make is not taking risks because they're too afraid of failure. This fear can lead to missed opportunities - and even if it doesn't, it stunts creativity and progress. Confidence allows us to embrace risk and make decisions with conviction. It helps us to take a chance and be resilient when things don't always go according to plan.

Not Taking Feedback Constructively

Unconfident people tend to let criticism bring them down, rather than use it as an opportunity for growth and improvement. They focus on the negative feedback instead of looking at what they can learn from it and adjust accordingly.Taking feedback constructively will help you become more confident in yourself and your abilities.

Not Being Open Minded

Unconfident people often give themselves limited choices due to the assumption that some are not achievable or too risky, which leads them to failing before even attempting something new or different. They miss out on chances to stand out by trying new approaches and exploring different possibilities that could potentially improve their overall success rate.

By avoiding these common mistakes made by unconfident people, you'll be better positioned to succeed in business. So take risks, listen to feedback with an open mindset, and you'll soon find yourself achieving more than ever before!

So, confidence plays a major role in success, and even the most successful business people may not realize the power of their own self-assurance. Confidence drives decision-making, presentation, and communication - qualities that, when combined together, form the perfect recipe for success. With practice and experience, anyone can build their confidence and become the best version of themselves in a professional setting.

Whether it's handling pressure, taking risks, making tough decisions, or speaking up in a meeting, confident people have the edge in tackling business challenges and coming out on top. As a result, it is important to cultivate self-confidence in order to propel yourself to success in the business world.

Chapter 4

Find Out about Yourself in Relation with Your Mission

Your Field of Expertise Should Determine What You Do

When you're trying to figure out how best to use your skills and talents, it can be difficult to decide on the right tasks to work on. You want to make sure that the work you are doing is aligned with your expertise and adds value in the right areas. But how do you determine what tasks are best suited for your skill set? It's a common challenge that can leave many feeling overwhelmed and uncertain as they try to make the most out of their abilities.

I am going to share my tips on why your field of expertise should drive your task selection in order to make sure that you are using your skills in the most effective way possible. By understanding the value of leveraging your expertise, you'll be able to create a task list that helps you get the most out of each day.

What Are the Benefits of Specialization?

In getting the most out of your skill set, specialization should be top of mind. It's easy to think that any task should be taken on no matter your expertise, but understand that doing so is a disservice to you and those around you.

By specializing in a certain piece of work or field, you can become an expert - able to handle complex tasks and bring quality results with confidence. Your specialized skill set will also make you more valuable and attractive to employers, as it will give you an edge over competition when applying for job openings.

When putting together your task list for the day or week, consider whether or not it falls in line with your expertise. That will help you showcase your unique capabilities and increase the likelihood of success - both professionally and personally.

Defining Your Skills and Areas of Expertise

In making the most out of your skill set, it's important that you first define what you are an expert in. Doing this will help you determine which tasks you should pursue and which ones you should leave for others to handle.

Take some time to consider what topics and skills come naturally for you as well as which areas challenge and engage you the most. You may find that there are certain tasks that require more effort than others and make it difficult to complete them in a timely manner. If there is something challenging that you know someone else can do better than you, then it's best to pass those tasks on.

Remember that expertise isn't limited to just one field. Consider any side skills or hobbies that could give you a competitive edge. Whether it's a knack for public speaking or an eye for design, take advantage of these assets and use them in new ways that would benefit your current tasks or future goals.

By defining your skillset and recognizing your unique areas of expertise, you can ensure that the tasks assigned to you fall within your wheelhouse - allowing you to do your best work efficiently and effectively.

Making Opportunities to Develop Your Expertise

When you already have expertise in an area, it would be a waste not to use it. Putting yourself in a place to make the most out of your skillset can give you the opportunity to grow and develop new ideas - and even help your career. Your field of expertise should determine your tasks so that you can make the most out of what you know.

Here are three ways you can use your expertise to create opportunities:

- **Leverage Your Skillset:** When planning projects or tasks, think about what skillsets and talents you bring to the table and how they could be used to solve the problem or get the task completed efficiently. This will give you a competitive edge in handling the job.
- **Take on Challenging Projects:** Look for projects that challenge your existing skills by pushing yourself into new areas and trying something different that builds on past successes. Aim for projects that require multiple skillsets and stretch across different areas of expertise so that you can grow in what you do.
- **Network with People in Your Field:** By networking with people who are also working in your field, you can create opportunities for developing new ideas, and learning from others' experiences in the same situation as yours - which will further expand your knowledge and capabilities. This will give you an advantage when tackling challenging tasks down the road.

Differentiating Between Tasks That Should Be Outsourced and Those You Should Take On

Sure, everyone has to fill their plate in order to meet expectations, but there are certain tasks that simply don't need to take up your time. That's where the wisdom of delegating comes in - you know what you're good at and what you enjoy doing, and outsourcing the rest makes a lot of sense.

But how can you differentiate between which tasks should be outsourced and those you should take on? The bottom line is basing off of your specific skill set - where do your strengths lie? What are the areas in which you can make the biggest impact?

Your Skillset

Identifying your skillset is the foundation for everything else; when the task comes in, ask yourself: "Is this something I am good at? Is this something I enjoy doing? Is this something I can do better than anyone else?" If not, it might be worth considering outsourcing.

Your Resources

Assess whether you have enough resources to take on a task yourself - if it's going to take up a significant portion of your time and energy, then it might be worth seeking help elsewhere. Consider whether it's feasible for someone else to do the job for you and weigh that against other obligations that come with doing it yourself.

At the end of the day, delegating work means elevating your skillset. You don't want to bog yourself down with too many tasks; if another person is better equipped to take them on than you are then go for it! It allows you to focus on what really matters - being part of making something great happen.

Why Hiring Professionals Is Also Essential to Specialization

It's easy to become overwhelmed when there are so many tasks to complete in a day, and that's why it is essential to hire professionals and focus on the tasks within your field of expertise. By hiring professionals, you can trust that work will be done correctly by those who specialize in the task. This means that you have the peace of mind knowing the job will be done properly and efficiently, but also enables you to focus on other areas where you have experience.

Moreover, specializing in a particular task or project allows for greater potential for growth in your career. For instance, if you're a professional writer who specializes in copywriting, then you can hone your skills and develop as an expert in this area. The same goes for any profession - by narrowing down your focus to just one field, you have more time to become an expert and increase your competence level.

Specialization gives you the ability to hone a specific skill set, more control over projects, ensures work is done correctly and efficiently, increases your chances of becoming an expert, and leads greater potential for career growth.

Setting Goals That Encourage Your Skill Development

What is the point of developing your skill set? It's all about setting goals that are achievable and that align with your expertise. When you have a goal in mind - whether it's to develop a new software program or to finish a project on time - you can use your skills and knowledge to get there.

If you're looking for a way to challenge yourself, try setting goals that require you to stretch your expertise and learn new things. This not only helps you hone the skills you already have, but also gives you an opportunity to gain new skills and become even more valuable in the workplace. Here are some steps you can take:

1. Identify areas of opportunity or growth - What do you want to learn or do differently?
2. Set realistic yet challenging deadlines - Make sure that your goals are achievable within the timeframe given.
3. Measure your progress against industry benchmarks - Are you meeting standards for success and proficiency?
4. Track short-term wins, such as projects completed on time - Showing yourself what is possible shows growth over time and encourages further learning opportunities.
5. Make sure you're focusing on long-term success - You'll need dedication and consistency to reach those big goals in the future.

By taking control of your skill development and setting these kinds of goals, you'll find yourself on track for even bigger successes down the line.

In assigning tasks to yourself, it's important to consider your expertise and skill sets. You should be taking on roles and tasks that use the skills that you have and help you learn new ones. Don't get stuck in a rut, and don't be afraid to challenge yourself with more difficult tasks.

Your tasks should reflect your interests and passions, so don't be afraid to take on something new. Challenge yourself, push yourself to learn and grow, and take pride in the work that you're doing. You are your own best asset, and your skill set is a part of that. Don't be afraid to make the most out of your skill set and see what you can achieve.

Don't Get into a Business You Don't Understand

You have a brilliant business idea and you're ready to get it up and running. But before you dive head first into the entrepreneurial pool, there are a few things you should consider so as not to get in over your head - literally and figuratively.

Starting any business comes with certain risks that should not be taken lightly. And one of the most important considerations is understanding the fundamentals of your chosen industry. If you don't understand all the angles of your proposed business, it will be extremely difficult to make informed decisions down the line and even more difficult to succeed in the long run.

We will look at some potential pitfalls that come with starting a business without being well-versed in its operations. With my help, you can gain an understanding of what to look out for so that you can start your business on firm footing and set yourself up for success.

When starting a business, it is vital to make sure you have a deep understanding of the industry you're entering into. Without proper knowledge of the industry, you'll find yourself quickly off track and unable to move forward.

For newbies, without knowing the ins-and-outs of your business, it makes it difficult to identify opportunities when they arise. Many businesses are successful because of their ability to seize on new opportunities for growth, but if you don't understand the business landscape, you won't be able to recognize which opportunities are worth taking and which ones are too risky.

Without a strong understanding of your industry and competitors embarking on similar initiatives, it's hard for entrepreneurs to accurately gauge their own progress. Market research takes on even more significance when you don't understand your product's competitive landscape and have no idea how to differentiate yourself from competitors who may be offering similar products or services.

In short, don't enter into a business venture blindly. Before starting a business venture of any kind - make sure that you have done your due diligence to gain a comprehensive understanding of the industry in order to set yourself up for success in the long run.

Identifying the Risks of Launching a Business Without Sufficient Knowledge

knowledge is power. Not having a full understanding of the business before you launch can be highly detrimental, as there are many risks associated with not knowing what you're getting into. Here are a few of the biggest potential pitfalls to take cognizance of:

- Not having a deep understanding of the industry and its regulations: Every industry has its own unique set of rules and regulations that must be kept in mind when running a business. Without a good grasp on them, there is no guarantee that your operations will remain compliant.
- Poor knowledge of customer needs: Knowing your customer is essential to creating an effective product or service that meets their needs. Without an accurate assessment of their wants and expectations,

- you may end up offering something that does not meet their needs or pique their interest.
- Inadequate understanding of competitor offerings: It's important to understand the competition within the market in order to stand out from them and create something better or different. If you don't have knowledge about what makes your competitors successful, then you may struggle to differentiate yourself from others in the market.

Having sufficient knowledge about all aspects of starting a business before beginning can help prevent potential pitfalls from occurring and save you both time and money in the long run.

Staying Informed and Being Able to Anticipate Changes in the Industry

It's often said that "ignorance is bliss", and while this might be true in some areas of life, it absolutely isn't in business. If you don't understand the ins and outs of the industry you want to get into, you're going to be in for a nasty surprise when something unexpected happens. There are ways to stay informed. For example, attending trade shows and industry conferences can keep you up-to-date with the latest trends, regulations and hot topics. You should also make sure that you regularly check all relevant websites for information on changes that could affect your business.

Again, don't forget about networking. This is an invaluable way for small business owners to build relationships with their peers and learn from them. Ultimately, these connections can help you anticipate any changes in the industry, so they can be addressed before they affect your business.

Need to Protect Yourself With Proper Legal Advice

It's not all that easy to launch a business if you don't fully understand the legal implications and regulations. The best way to protect your business is by making sure you have the right legal advice.

Why Get Legal Advice?

Getting legal advice allows you to cover any bases that could impact your business later on down the line. Whether it's registering trademarks, understanding tax requirements or even dealing with customers and suppliers - getting professional advice from a lawyer can help give your business an edge and get it off to a great start.

The earlier the better - you want to make sure you are legally compliant and protected from the very beginning. A lawyer can help you with everything from setting up contracts to forming LLCs or partnerships, so make sure to speak with one before entering into any arrangements or agreements with anyone else.

By enlisting the services of a lawyer, you will ensure that:

- Your contracts are airtight
- Your rights as a business owner are protected
- You are complying with relevant laws
- You have someone on hand who can provide informed insight when needed
- You won't be inadvertently exposed to risk in the course of doing business

Starting a business without truly understanding it may not be the best idea, but that doesn't mean you cannot still become successful as a business owner. Be sure to take your time to learn as much as you can, gather resources and take advantage of any opportunity to collaborate with others who may have more experience. Doing your due diligence and taking precautions can help ensure that you have a successful and rewarding venture without the potential pitfalls of inexperience.

Chapter 5

Stay Focused

How an Entrepreneur Can Apply Focus for Business Success

As an entrepreneur, you likely spend a great deal of your time and energy on research, strategizing, pitching, and dealing with the day-to-day of starting and running a business. With all that's involved in being an entrepreneur, it can be hard to maintain focus on a single task or goal. But if there's one key to success as an entrepreneur, it's having the ability to stay focused. Being able to concentrate on one task at a time can help you manage your workload more efficiently, find solutions to pressing problems faster, and maximize productivity - no matter how demanding the situation gets.

Understanding What Focus Is and Why It Is Important

Focus is the ability to direct your attention and energy on a single task and stay on task without getting distracted. Whether you're working with clients directly, managing finances or preparing for an upcoming launch, having laser focus can help you get the job done more efficiently.

Having sharp focus has many advantages. It helps you be productive by freeing up mental energy from worry and other distractions, creates a sense of purpose that allows you to optimize your time, and gives you the ability to maintain clarity and concentrate on what's important in order to reach your goals.

Focus also helps reduce stress levels since you don't waste your mental resources on worrying about things you can't control. Instead, by focusing on one specific task at a time, it will help keep your mind clear and organized so that when it comes time to tackle bigger projects or goals, you know exactly how to break them down into manageable tasks that are easier to finish.

The Benefits of Having a Focused Mindset

You may have heard it said that time is the most valuable resource, but really, what's more important is how you use that time. Having a focused mindset can be the difference between success and failure in realizing your business dreams.

Staying focused on a single task sends a strong signal to your brain that it is important and worth dedicating attention to, and this can help you accomplish goals faster. This level of focus also allows for better problem-solving and creativity, enabling you to come up with solutions that you may not have been able to think of otherwise. Additionally, being able to stay focused on tasks helps you become more organized and effective in managing multiple projects.

The most important thing is to set realistic goals for the future and break them down into smaller, achievable steps. This allows your mind to stay on track and make steady progress towards achieving your overall goal. When distractions arise, make sure to quickly address them and move back into focus mode so as not to lose momentum. By implementing regular 'focus times' throughout the day, you will be sure to stay productive and motivated in achieving your goals.

Setting Achievable Goals

Setting achievable goals is one of the best strategies for staying focused. Goals that are realistic and attainable are essential when it comes to keeping focus and succeeding in business.

When establishing goals, it's important to define what success looks like. A good goal should be Specific, Measurable, Achievable, Relevant and Time-bound (SMART). For example, instead of having a goal of "increasing sales", set a more specific goal such as "achieving 10% increase in sales within the next 3 months." This helps you stay focused on taking meaningful steps and working towards success over time.

In addition, breaking down large goals into smaller ones can help you stay motivated and on track. By focusing on individual tasks necessary to accomplish the larger goal, you can maintain consistent motivation rather than trying to tackle the entire project at once. This will also help keep your focus on the immediate task or steps that need to be taken in order to reach your bigger goal.

Growing Your Network Wisely

You know the old saying - "Your network is your net worth" - it's so true. Growing your network wisely is one of the best strategies for staying focused. Building relationships with like-minded people can really help when you need guidance and support to reach your goals. Plus, having a network of supportive professionals helps keep you motivated when times get tough.

Finding Your Tribe

Finding, building and maintaining relationships is critical to business success. It's essential to take time out of your busy schedule to cultivate relationships with people who have similar ambitions and ideals as yourself. This could be through joining groups who share common goals, attending industry events, or even just reaching out to friends and family for support!

And remember, not all relationships are created equal. It's important to carefully choose which people and organizations you want in your network - be sure to connect with those who will add value to you in some way - whether that's knowledge, skills or even moral support!

A strong network will help bring visibility to your business and build credibility for the long run – something that a successful entrepreneur needs.

Develop an Action Plan and Accountability System

Maintaining focus is a key factor in business success. As an entrepreneur, what can you do to stay focused and reach the goals you set? It all comes down to having an action plan and accountability system.

Create an Action Plan

An action plan consists of breaking down your objectives into smaller, actionable steps. Determine what needs to be accomplished each day and give yourself a timeline for completing each step. This not only provides clarity of purpose but helps prevent overwhelm or procrastination.

Hold Yourself Accountable

Now that you have your action plan, set measurable benchmarks along the way so that you can track your progress and make changes if needed. Sticking to deadlines is key, but don't be too hard on yourself if you don't reach them - simply adjust your timeline as needed.

Find Support Resources

It's also important to find support resources like coaches, mentors and fellow entrepreneurs who can help you stay on track with your goals. Having someone to turn to when things get tough will keep you motivated, provide a different perspective on tricky challenges, and increase the chances of success.

Optimizing Time Management Habits and Practices

Maintaining focus as an entrepreneur is closely related to effective time management and optimization of your habits and practices. Putting a few essential strategies into place can help you make the most of your time, stay on track, and move closer to business success.

Set a Schedule

Establish a routine by setting a daily schedule that allows you to maximize focus and productivity. When it comes to time blocking, the goal is not to fill the entire day with activities, but rather prioritize tasks that are essential for the day's success. This helps you avoid getting distracted by other tasks that are not related to your current goal.

Establish Rules for Interruptions

Allow yourself frequent breaks throughout the day and set rules for interruptions. Let people around you know when they can expect your response or availability - this could be during specific hours, or through communication platforms like email or chat platforms like Slack. It is also important not to let digital distractions get in the way of productivity; disable notifications and resist the urge of turning off task-related notifications or switching tabs when working on an assignment or project.

Stick To Deadlines

Before taking on any project, identify what needs to be done within what time frame so you don't find yourself lagging behind when approaching deadlines. For larger projects, it might be helpful to break down tasks into smaller subtasks so that it's easier for you to complete them within their specified timeframe. Additionally, managing expectations with clients from the start allows them to adhere to deadlines as well, ultimately helping both parties stay focused towards completion of projects on-time.

As an entrepreneur, staying focused is the key to success. Taking time to plan, work on impulse control, practice mindfulness, and set goals can help entrepreneurs to stay focused on what matters most and achieve their goals. This allows them to maximize their time and resources to reach their full potential.

Staying focused requires discipline and dedication but it can also be incredibly rewarding. Applying the strategies discussed above can help entrepreneurs to stay focused on their goals and create a successful business. By doing so, they can create a legacy that can last for generations to come.

The Bottom up Focus System: How It Can Help You Achieve Your Goals

Achieving our goals is not always easy. We set out with the best of intentions, but then somewhere along the way, we get stuck in a rut and fail to reach our destination. Focusing on the big picture can be overwhelming and discouraging - so why not take a different approach?

Enter the bottom up focus system. This system keeps you motivated by breaking your goal into smaller, achievable steps that you can check off as you go along. It takes a little planning, but it's an incredibly effective way to keep your progress steady and manageable.

We will look into how this approach works and how you can apply it to your own goals.

Exploring the Basics of the Bottom Up Focus System

If you're looking for a reliable way to achieve your goals, the bottom up focus system may be the solution you've been searching for. It helps to break down your goals into manageable, achievable steps that build on each other - which is why it's often referred to as a "bottom up" approach. It starts with focusing on the basics and gradually leads you to reach new heights of success.

Let's put this concept in practice. Imagine that you have a goal of running a marathon. To begin with, you'll need to focus on building up your strength and endurance with smaller, more attainable objectives such as walking around the block or running a few miles every day. As you start to check off those milestones, you'll have an easier time when it comes time for your marathon run because your body will already be used to working out and pushing its limits.

Overall, the bottom up focus system gives structure and direction needed for almost any goal. And with determination and consistency in mind, it can help guide anyone toward reaching their highest potential and becoming successful in whatever they set out to do!

Identifying Your Goals

Achieving your goals is all about taking those first steps - and with the bottom up focus system, you can make sure that those steps are meaningful ones. This system encourages you to start small, then build on that momentum until you've not only identified your goals but created a plan to achieve them.

Want to run a marathon? Start by setting a smaller goal - train for a 10k, then a half-marathon, and so on. Or maybe you're aiming for something more academic or professional like getting your Master's degree or launching your own business. Again, the bottom up focus system helps you break large projects into smaller mini goals so they don't seem too overwhelming.

Start by getting in the right mindset by writing down one thing you would like to achieve in the next 6 months. You'll soon find that this helps you stay focused and motivated as you work towards it - and eventually onto bigger and better things!

Breaking Down Goals Into Bite-Sized Pieces

One of the most effective techniques for achieving your goals is to break them down into bite-sized pieces that are easier to accomplish. With the Bottom Up Focus System, you can do just that!

The Bottom Up Focus System helps you create a clear path to achieving your goals by breaking them down into smaller, achievable chunks. This allows you to focus on one step at a time and make progress towards success in a manageable way.

Instead of taking on a goal as one large task, breaking it down into smaller pieces allows you to prioritize and focus on what needs to be done first. Each step then becomes like its own mini-goal, making it easier to stay motivated throughout the process. You'll also be able to track your progress more effectively since you'll know exactly what steps need to be taken and which tasks have been completed.

This type of structure can help keep things organized and allow you to stay focused on your ultimate goal even when faced with challenges or roadblocks along the way. With the Bottom Up Focus System, you can maximize your chances of success by taking small steps towards achieving your ambitions!

Setting an Action Plan for Your Goals

When setting out to achieve your goals, an important part of the process is creating an action plan. The bottom up focus system gives you a foolproof way to do that - it takes the strategy and vision of your ultimate goal and breaks it down into manageable steps, giving you a road map to success.

This 'bottom up' approach starts with a clear vision of your end goal, then works its way backwards by breaking that goal into smaller objectives. From there, these objectives can be broken down even further into actionable tasks that will help you get to where you want to be.

By starting with an achievable 'big picture', and then breaking it down into smaller components, it's easy to prioritize what needs to be done first and come up with an effective timeline for your goals. This can help you stay organized and accountable, since each task is essentially a stepping stone leading towards the bigger picture.

What's more, this bottom up focus system allows for continual progress tracking: by regularly assessing where you have reached in relation to your goals, any milestones achieved or obstacles faced along the way can be tracked for future reference. This means that you can adjust any elements of your plan as needed so that each task is completed at the right time and in the right way.

By utilizing the bottom up focus system as part of your goal-setting process, breaking big projects down into smaller tasks becomes much simpler. As a result, by setting yourself achievable steps along the way, successful completion of ultimate goals becomes more likely than ever before.

Monitoring Your Progress and Making Adjustments

If you want to reach new heights and reach your goals, you need to have a plan - a plan with milestones and checkpoints so you can track and monitor your progress. After all, if you don't measure it, it's not real.

The bottom up focus system is the perfect tool for this. It helps you stay on top of things by setting achievable milestones and objectives, breaking down complex tasks into manageable chunks that are easy to measure and monitor. It also allows for adjusting goals if needed as new information becomes available.

To make the most of this system:

- Start small with short-term objectives. This will give you a starting point for measuring success and provide a foundation of confidence as you make progress towards bigger goals.
- Break down bigger objectives into smaller tasks that can be completed more quickly, making them easier to manage and track better over time.
- Monitor progress by keeping track of how far you've come and how close you are to achieving your goal so that adjustments can be made if necessary when unexpected obstacles arise or when new information becomes available.

The Pattern of Celebrating Success and Gaining Momentum

With the bottom up focus system, you can break down your goals into smaller, achievable steps and keep your momentum going.

A significant part of achieving your goals is recognizing when you take a step in the right direction. Celebrating successes along the way helps you stay motivated and encourages you to keep pushing forward. How do you celebrate success?

- **Make it public:** Share your successes with people close to you or on social media - this helps validate what you've done and will inspire others as well!
- **Turn up the volume:** Give yourself permission to really embrace this moment - call a friend, turn up the music, and do whatever else makes you feel joyous.
- **Take note:** Keep track of everything that has gone right in order to remind yourself what is possible when you put your mind to it.
- **Reward yourself:** Treating yourself for reaching key milestones can reinforce good behaviors and help maintain forward motion towards bigger goals.

So go ahead and celebrate those wins, no matter how small they may seem - it will help drive your goal-achieving momentum!

In summary, no matter the outcome, the bottom up focus system is a great way to create structure, prioritize tasks, and stay accountable for progress. It allows you to identify smaller steps on the way to bigger goals, and by breaking them down into tangible components, you can stay motivated and reach new heights in your life, career, and business.

By not just focusing on the big picture, but on the fine details that come with it, your goals become more tangible and achievable. With the bottom up focus system, you can set yourself up for success and reach both short-term and long-term accomplishments, while staying mindful and in control of your journey.

Golf: A Subtle Mystery of Business Focus

Golf has been a popular sport for decades, with many people playing for the sheer joy of it. However, golf is also a sport that can help you in your career. It is a game that requires immense focus, discipline, patience, and strategy - qualities that are also essential in the business world.

Playing golf can be a fantastic way to build relationships and network with colleagues, clients, and potential clients. It can also help you to relax and unwind from the stress of the office, allowing you to come back to work with renewed focus and energy.

I want you to discover how golf can benefit your business, the benefits of playing golf, the skills it requires, and the strategies you can use to make the most of your time on the course while you continue your business.

Golf has long been known as a sport of business professionals, with many deals being closed on the greens. But what is it about golf that makes it such a popular choice for networking and building business relationships?

One reason is the time commitment required to play a round of golf. It's not a quick game that can be played during a lunch break – it can take several hours to complete. This gives players ample time to get to know each other, discuss business matters and build rapport.

Another reason is the nature of the game itself. Golf requires a great deal of focus and concentration, particularly when putting. It also involves strategy and planning, as players must navigate the course and choose the right clubs for each shot. These skills translate well to the business world, where focus, strategy, and planning are also essential for success.

Again, golf provides a relaxed and informal setting for business interactions. The pressure and formality of a boardroom meeting are replaced with the camaraderie of playing a round of golf. This can help to build trust and foster positive relationships between business partners.

The connection between golf and business is clear. Whether it's networking, building relationships, or improving focus and strategic thinking, golf can be a valuable tool for business professionals looking to boost their success.

Can the Sport Help Improve Focus and Concentration?

Golf is a game that requires a lot of focus and concentration. From the moment you step onto the course, you need to be aware of your surroundings and the conditions of the course. You need to be able to focus on each shot and make adjustments based on the conditions and the position of the ball. This level of focus and concentration can be beneficial in business as well.

When you're in the boardroom, you need to be able to concentrate on the task at hand and not be distracted by other things going on around you. You need to be able to focus on the details and make decisions based on the information presented to you. This is where golf can help.

Through playing golf regularly, you can improve your ability to focus and concentrate. You'll become more aware of your surroundings and be able to make adjustments based on the conditions around you. This can translate into the boardroom where you'll be able to focus on the task at hand and make decisions based on the information presented to you.

Golf can also help with stress management. The game can be frustrating at times, but being able to stay calm and focused can help you manage stress in other areas of your life. This can be especially beneficial in business where stress levels can be high. It can be a great way to improve focus and concentration, which can translate into better decision-making skills and stress management in the boardroom.

The Parallels between Golf and Business Strategy

Golf and business strategy have many parallels that can be drawn. In golf, you cannot control the weather or the course conditions, but you can control your mindset and strategy. Similarly, in business, you cannot control the competition or the market conditions, but you can control your own strategy and focus.

Both golf and business require planning, focus, and execution. In golf, you need to plan your shots, concentrate on the ball, and execute your swing. In business, you need to plan your goals, concentrate on your tasks, and execute your strategy.

Moreover, both golf and business require patience and perseverance. In golf, you may hit a bad shot or have a bad hole, but you need to stay focused and continue to play. In business, you may face setbacks or failures, but you need to stay motivated and persevere.

In addition, golf and business require continuous improvement. In golf, you need to practice your swing and technique to become better. In business, you need to learn from your mistakes and continuously improve your strategy and skills.

By understanding these parallels between golf and business strategy, individuals can use golf as a tool to enhance their business focus and performance.

So, golf is not just a sport, it's an excellent tool that can help improve focus and productivity in the boardroom. By incorporating golf into your business routine, you can gain a competitive edge over your peers and enhance your networking capabilities.

To get started, consider joining a local golf club or booking a lesson with a professional coach. You can also explore business networking events that involve golf, such as charity tournaments or corporate outings.

Remember that while golf can be a fun and relaxing activity, it's also important to approach it with a strategic mindset. Use the game as an opportunity to sharpen your focus, develop better communication skills, and build relationships with colleagues and clients.

Chapter 6

Learn from Experience

Success Is Hidden in Past Failures

Did you know that success and failure are two sides of the same coin? The world, we've been taught, has a natural order - an order that demands failure before success can be truly achieved. As difficult as it may be to accept, it's true: sometimes setbacks are an essential part of success.

If you're looking to achieve something in life, it's easy to become intimidated by the idea of failure. But you don't have to be. Instead, look at failure differently.

We will consider it a necessary part of success - something that can help us learn and grow into the person we want to be. You will see why failure is often essential for success and how learning from our mistakes can propel us onto bigger and better things.

Identifying Your Past Failures

We've all gone through moments of failure in our lives, but it's what we do afterwards that defines our character. Learning from your past failures can help you become better prepared for the obstacles you will encounter in life and give you the strength and courage to continue striving for success.

When looking back on your failures, it's important to identify them first. Acknowledging what didn't work out in the past helps you gain a better understanding of why it happened and how it can affect your future goals. It's also essential to take full responsibility for what happened – no one is perfect, but taking ownership of your mistakes shows an admirable strength and sets a good example for those around you.

Once you recognize your shortcomings, it is easier to determine how to develop strategies that will help you succeed in the future. Use this as an opportunity to learn from your experiences and build on them – think through different approaches and out-of-the-box solutions that can steer you back in the right direction. With hard work and perseverance, these mistakes can become valuable lessons that can make all the difference along the journey towards success.

Uncovering the Lessons Learned from Your Failures

Failing isn't fun. It makes you feel helpless and lost, like you're stuck in a dark hole with no way out. But you need to remember that failure is an essential part of life. Every failure is an opportunity to learn, grow, and become better prepared for the future.

When reflecting on a past failure, try to uncover the lessons within it. Ask yourself what could have been done differently and what measurable steps could you have taken beforehand? What did you discover about yourself or the situation that made it a challenge?

Learning from your failures is the best way to use them as stepping stones to success. Acknowledge any mistakes made and use those lessons to set yourself up for future success - whether it's personal growth or financial gain. And don't forget: no matter how hard things seem right now, tomorrow is always a new day and a fresh start.

Contemplating How Your Failures Have Helped Shape Who You Are Today

You've failed many times in the past, but with each failure, you have gained knowledge and wisdom that can help you succeed in the future. Take some time to reflect on your failures and think about how they have shaped who you are today. What lessons have you learned? How has your experience with failure changed your outlook on life?

Reflection and Evaluation

Reflecting on your failures allows you to recognize patterns that have led to unsuccessful attempts and become aware of what will not work in the future. Evaluating these failures also allows you to identify ways in which you can improve or change your approach to better fit your goals. Knowing what has not worked gives a better idea of what could potentially work.

Embracing Failure

Failure is an opportunity for growth and learning, so it's important to embrace it instead of running away from it. When things don't go as planned, look for ways to turn those failures into successes: look for solutions, ask yourself how can this be done differently, or how can I fix this issue? Doing so will increase your ability to learn from mistakes and gain valuable insight into approaching problems differently.

Start looking at failure as a challenge for personal growth and use it as an opportunity for self-improvement rather than something to be feared. Embracing failure will help develop resilience and allow future successes.

Re-Framing Your Perspective to Find Success in Failures

Experiencing failure can be really tough, but it doesn't need to be all doom and gloom. By changing your perspective, you can find success even in failure. It all comes down to reframing the situation and understanding that, while there may have been a negative outcome, there are still positives to take away.

Here are some ways you can re-frame your perspective to gain success from failure:

Acknowledge that you failed

You may feel embarrassed or ashamed of the decisions that led up to the failure, but accepting and admitting that you have failed is a crucial step towards learning from it.

Take responsibility

Taking responsibility for the outcomes of your mistakes will help you to take ownership of what happened, instead of blaming someone else.

Reflect on why it happened

Reflecting on why it happened is an important part of gaining valuable insight from a failure. Ask yourself questions like "What could I have done differently?" and "What did I learn from this experience?"

Celebrate positive action taken

It may seem counter-intuitive, but celebrating positive action taken can help you find success in failures. Celebrating how far you've come and how many obstacles you've managed to overcome is a great way to motivate yourself during difficult times.

By re-framing failures within a more positive outlook, you will be able to take valuable lessons away and build your confidence for future successes.

Breaking Down the Barriers of Fear in Order to Take Risks

At this point in the process, you need to break down the barriers you have that are keeping you from taking risks. Understand that failure is not an indicator of future success and actually can be just the opposite. The basic idea here is to look for positive life lessons in each failed experience and keep your eyes on the prize.

But how do you actually break down these barriers?

1. Realize that risk-taking can be beneficial and understand that the worst outcome is rarely as bad as you think it will be.
2. Remind yourself of all of your successes rather than dwelling on your failures - it's easier to take risks when you have a history of success.
3. Celebrate every small step forward, no matter how small it may seem - that will encourage you to take more risks in the future.
4. Don't let fear stop you from reaching your goals and if you fail, use it as a learning opportunity and remember that failure is part of the process.
5. Surround yourself with people who will support you in taking risks and help lift your spirits if things don't work out immediately as planned.

When you recognize your ability to learn from each mistake and using this knowledge to inform future decisions, you can use past failures as stepping stones towards success.

Moving Forward Towards Success With a Fresh Mindset

The key to learning from your past failures is to move forward towards success with a fresh mindset. It can be easy to be bogged down by the failures and experience a lack of motivation or confidence to continue trying, but it's important to remember that these setbacks are part of the process and should be embraced in order to learn from them.

Taking a step back from the situation and evaluating what went wrong can help you gain perspective into what changes need to be made for you to achieve success in the future. So, how do you move forward?

- Don't dwell on the negatives - Focus on what you learned and how you will use this knowledge towards future successes.

- Create a plan - Create an actionable plan that maps out how you will overcome the current setback and leverage this experience into achieving success in the future.
- Remain motivated - Set realistic goals, reward yourself along the way, and celebrate even small wins along your journey - this will help keep you motivated as you move towards success!

By learning from past experiences, staying motivated, and creating an actionable plan, you can move forward towards success with a fresh mindset and ultimately reach greater heights than before.

Although failure can be painful, it can also be a powerful teacher. Learning from our past mistakes, and using that knowledge to inform our future decisions, can help us achieve the success we are seeking. The path to success may not always be easy or straightforward, but with a clear understanding of our past, and an eagerness to persevere, we can reach our goals. Don't get discouraged by failure - embrace it as a stepping stone to success.

Everyone's had their fair share of setbacks in life. It's no different in business, and yet there are still those who find success despite the hiccups and obstacles. But what is it that sets them apart? How do they turn failure into triumph?

I believe that the answer lies in the insight of some of the most successful businessmen around: Those who have faced adversity, learned from their mistakes, and used those lessons as fuel to spur themselves and their businesses on to greater heights.

Let me show you some of the most high-profile examples of successful businessmen who broke barriers by facing their personal failings head-on. Armed with this knowledge, you too can succeed despite the setbacks you may encounter.

No matter your industry, everyone can take inspiration from the successes of Warren Buffett, Steve Jobs, and Mark Zuckerberg. Each have unique stories that demonstrate how to overcome setbacks and persevere despite challenges.

Let's start with Warren Buffett, who famously began his career with a failed partnership before going on to become one of the world's most successful investors. By learning from his mistakes and understanding risk/reward investing, he developed an investment style that has earned him billions of dollars over the years.

Then there's Steve Jobs, who was famously fired from Apple in 1985 only to be re-hired and steer the company towards unprecedented success in the tech world. Drawing on lessons he learned while away from the company, Jobs was able to lead Apple to new heights while also revolutionizing consumer technology.

One can also look at Facebook CEO Mark Zuckerberg as an example of someone who faced adversity head-on but still managed to rise above it all. After various legal disputes and other controversies surrounding Facebook's growth, Zuckerberg has navigated a path forward that has kept Facebook as one of the preeminent tech giants for years now.

These three businessmen have demonstrated that success does not have to come easy; instead, it can be achieved by learning from failures and staying resilient despite obstacles in the path ahead.

I must emphasize that the best way to succeed is not to be afraid of making mistakes. Think of every mistake as an opportunity to learn and grow. By understanding and learning from our mistakes, we can avoid making the same mistakes in the future. This is something that successful businessmen have used to their advantage.

Take for example the success stories of Warren Buffett, Steve Jobs and Bill Gates. All three of these businessmen experienced set backs in their careers but used those experiences as learning opportunities. Buffett lost his first investment and was able to turn it into a positive by using what he learned from that mistake when investing going forward.

Similarly, Jobs and Gates were both fired from companies they founded but were able to learn from their mistakes and use that knowledge in their future successes.

The key takeaway here is not to be afraid of making mistakes - instead, use them as an opportunity to gain knowledge and experience that you can use for future success. By applying this wisdom, you too can follow in the footsteps of these popular businessmen who broke barriers and achieved success despite their setbacks.

The Importance of Perseverance and Resilience

It's no secret that there's no easy route to success. The successful businessmen you hear about all had to face setbacks, and they all found a way to persevere and rise above those obstacles. What this means is that perseverance and resilience are key characteristics for successful business people.

Not only do these feelings of resilience help you keep going through challenging times, but it also helps create a positive attitude, which is key when it comes to dealing with setbacks. This can be seen in the stories of several businessmen who have overcome a number of difficult circumstances - despite the odds being stacked against them.

Staying Positive in the Face of Failure

Failure doesn't define you; instead, it can bring valuable lessons if you're open-minded and willing to learn from it. Keeping a positive outlook on both successes and failures will give you the strength to move forward and turn your dreams into reality - just like these popular businessmen did in the face of adversity.

Learning how to take advantage of unexpected situations is a skill that some business people naturally possess. Setbacks can be seen as learning experiences, which can equip you with valuable skills such as problem-solving, creativity and strategic planning. Additionally, understanding how failures happened allows you to strategize around them and create better work-processes for future projects or businesses.

These popular businessmen have shown us that success isn't about avoiding failure; it's about learning from it and pushing forward despite the odds stacked against us - without giving up.

It's inspiring to learn about the success stories of popular businessmen despite all their setbacks. As you can see, the theme that runs through all of these stories is that the whole point of failing is to learn from it and keep going.

So what lessons can be learned from these stories?

Don't be discouraged by failure

No matter how often you fail, don't give up. Many of the popular businessmen we've looked at faced multiple rejections and failures, but they kept going and eventually achieved success.

Learn from your mistakes

Failing can be a difficult experience, but often it's exactly what we need to spur us on to greater heights. Each time it happens, think critically and analyze where you went wrong. That helps you avoid making the same mistakes again in future and also make better business decisions.

Think outside the box

Successful entrepreneurs are often creative thinkers who come up with new solutions to existing problems or develop innovative products or services that break away from conventions. Don't be afraid to experiment and take risks - you never know what might come out of it.

Understand their stories and take away valuable lessons. You too can reach success by learning from failure and ultimately breaking through any barriers that stand in your way. No matter what setbacks life throws your way, you can use them to develop a better, more resilient version of yourself. The lives of these businessmen serve as an example of how to persevere and learn from failure, in order to become successful.

No one's journey is easy and that's why it's so important to take some time to evaluate, analyze, and reflect on the obstacles you're up against. This will help you become a more strategic thinker and set yourself on a valuable path to success. So don't get discouraged by hardships, use them to your advantage and build a stronger, better version of yourself.

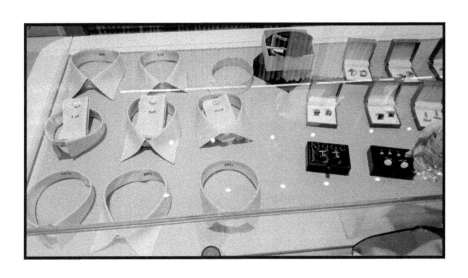

CHAPTER 7

Make a New Flexible Plan and Adjust It as You Move on

The Advantage of Flexible Business Plans

Life is full of unexpected twists and turns, and so is business. As a business owner, you know that success often hinges on the ability to adapt to changing times. That's why having a flexible business plan can make all the difference for your venture.

When you're stuck in a rigid plan or framework that doesn't allow for changes or revisions, it can be difficult - and maybe even impossible - to move with the times. A flexible plan, on the other hand, allows you to adjust and pivot when needed. It gives you the opportunity to seize unexpected opportunities and weather potentially turbulent situations.

I will explain why having a flexible plan is beneficial to any business - and provide some examples of how businesses have successfully implemented their own flexible plans in their pursuit of success.

What Is a Flexible Business Plan?

Do you want to take your business to the next level? If so, it's time to start thinking about flexibility. When it comes to a successful business, having a flexible plan is vital. But what exactly is a flexible business plan?

Essentially, this type of planning involves having the ability to adapt in order to get the most out of changing situations. Having a flexibility mindset and being quick on your feet helps businesses stay ahead of their competitors and the constantly evolving market conditions.

With a flexible plan, you have the ability to respond quickly and adjust when needed, rather than being tied down to rigid timelines and set strategies that may no longer be relevant or applicable as time goes on. In addition, it allows for innovating new solutions and real-time decision-making that ultimately result in success.

Benefits of Having a Flexible Business Plan

You might be wondering why you would want to have such a flexible business plan in place. The answer is simple: a well-crafted and flexible business plan gives you the freedom to pivot when necessary, allowing your organization to stay on top of changing trends, adapt to an ever-changing market, and make the most of new opportunities.

It also gives you the ability to respond quickly to unexpected challenges or sudden growth, so that your organization can keep up with shifting demand from customers or the introduction of new products.

Furthermore, a flexible business plan makes it easier for you to identify gaps in your processes and address them as they come up. This allows you to constantly evaluate and refine your performance, so that you can ensure optimal performance across all areas of your business.

Ultimately, having a flexible business plan ensures that you can stay ahead of the curve and maximize your return on investment in the long run - all while helping you adapt easily and effectively as the market continues to change.

Identifying Gaps in Traditional Business Plans

You may be familiar with traditional business plans, but have you ever considered the gaps they bring to the table?

Lack of Agility

Traditional business plans tend to be rigid and inflexible, so they can't adjust quickly enough when things change. This can severely limit your organization's competitiveness and ability to stay ahead of the curve. As any successful businessperson knows, being able to anticipate and respond swiftly to rapid changes in the marketplace is key - traditional planning just can't keep up with fast-moving markets.

Limited Creativity

Traditional plans also lack creativity, failing to accommodate innovative ideas or projects outside of established parameters. This almost guarantees that companies relying solely on traditional methods are stuck with outdated strategies that don't move them forward. By contrast, a flexible plan encourages creative ideas from all areas of your organization, leading you quickly toward new opportunities and growth potential.

Insufficient Feedback Loops

Another major issue with a static plan is that it doesn't allow for regular feedback loops and subsequent adjustments. Without continual review and improvement, your organization are missing out on huge opportunities for success as conditions in the market evolve. At best this leads to stagnation; at worst it could lead to failure if competitors overtake you due to insufficient adaptation.

A flexible business plan offers better solutions than traditional plans when it comes to agile response time, creative approaches and feedback loops - all essential elements of success in competitive markets today.

Strategies for Implementing a Flexible Business Plan

A flexible business plan is an amazing strategy for success in the modern world, so it's important to know how to implement one. Here are a few tips for getting started:

Set Organizational Goals

Make sure you have clear organizational goals that everyone in your team is aware of and understands. No matter how quickly things change, these core objectives will remain the same and can be used as a guide for making decisions in rapidly-evolving markets.

Monitor Your Progress

To make sure you stay on track, monitor your progress regularly. Take account of what works and what doesn't. If something isn't working, don't be afraid to change it. This could mean taking on different strategies or adjusting timelines to reach your goals - both of which are easier with a flexible plan.

Involve Teams & Customers

Involve your teams and customers in any decision-making processes that affect them or their workflows. Additionally, use customer feedback to adapt your products or services when necessary. This not only helps build loyalty but makes sure that your business remains relevant to customers' needs - a vital aspect of staying competitive in today's markets.

What Can You Do to Ensure Your Plan Stays Flexible?

Achieving success with a flexible plan starts with an open mind. You must be willing to adapt your business plan as needed or risk becoming outdated and irrelevant. How do you get this done?

Prioritize Agility

Make sure that everyone involved in the plan is working toward the same goal and understands why agility is important. This ensures they stay focused on their tasks, even during times of change.

Review Regularly

Regularly review your plans to ensure they are up-to-date and relevant to current trends and circumstances. It ensures that changes are implemented and adjustments made quickly, so your plans remain flexible and responsive.

Leverage Technology

Make use of technology, such as cloud-based tools, to easily update plans and keep track of changes. It helps you stay ahead of the competition by quickly making adjustments as needed.

Ensure you remain aware of changes in the market, trends in customer needs, and what works in your particular industry. You'll be better equipped to make timely decisions that keep the business plan flexible when the environment shifts around you.

What Are the Common Pitfalls With Flexible Business Plans?

Flexible business plans are great - but there are some common pitfalls you should be aware of.

Being overly optimistic

For starters, it's easy to get overly optimistic when making your flexible plan. You may think that all future plans and prospects will prove successful, and that can set you up for failure if things don't turn out as you expect them to. It's important to be realistic in making your flexible plan and understand that things might not always go as planned.

Not creating enough structure

Another pitfall when it comes to flexible business plans is not creating enough structure. Flexible business plans should still have expectations, timelines, and metrics in place to help keep the team on track. Without having more rigid points of reference, the team may slip into a disorganized state which can lead to less productivity overall.

Too rigid

A lot of people don't realize that a flexible business plan can become too rigid if it's not regularly adjusted or revised in response to customer feedback or changes in the market. If you're unable to change or modify your business plan as needed, then it can quickly turn from being agile and responsive into something rigid and outdated - which defeats the purpose entirely!

To avoid these pitfalls and make sure your flexible business plan is truly successful, make sure to stay mindful of expectations for yourself and your team, create structures for reference and accountability, and regularly adjust according to customer feedback or changing market conditions.

Finally, having a flexible business plan allows for adaptable growth that can adjust to the ever-changing business environment. It requires an entrepreneurial spirit and the ability to quickly pivot and take advantage of any new opportunities that present themselves.

Being able to respond to change with openness and agility will give you the confidence to take calculated risks and keep your business ahead of the competition. Moving with the times and keeping up with the current trends and developments in your industry are essential for success.

A flexible business plan is not just about having the right strategies, but also having the right attitude and mindset to embrace change and use it to your advantage. By being open to new ideas and recognizing how and when to adapt your business plan to suit the current environment, you can ensure the long-term sustainability and success of your business.

A Lesson from Popular Businesses which Failed Due to Rigid Business Plans

As a business owner, you know that it's essential to have good plans and procedures in place. That's why it's so important to make sure they are flexible enough to adapt when the need arises. Unfortunately, not all businesses get this right.

There are countless examples of businesses that failed due to inflexible planning. From the famous failure of Blockbuster Video in the face of streaming services, to the rise and fall of Atari with its failure to diversify and stay ahead of the competition. The stories are varied, but there's one common thread: That sticking to a rigid plan could have very dire consequences.

Let's take a closer look at some popular businesses that failed due to inflexible planning and what we can learn from their costly mistakes.

Perhaps you've got a plan and you're sticking to it, no matter what. If that's the case, then you need to know about inflexible business plans - and how they can lead to major failure.

Inflexible business plans are ones that don't change - even when the market does. They don't incorporate new industry trends, or account for changes in customer preference and demand. This of course can be incredibly costly for businesses, as we've seen with so many famous companies that failed due to their rigid approach.

Take for example Blockbuster Video, which refused to embrace the changing times by not adapting to digital streaming services like Netflix; or Kodak, who refused to acknowledge the demand for digital photography solutions; and Borders Books, who could have survived if they had embraced e-commerce sooner.

Inflexible planning means playing catch-up instead of staying ahead - but by understanding its potential impact on your business, you can make sure it doesn't become your downfall.

Kodak: Mistaking the Market for a Camera

The greatest danger of a rigid business plan is that it can cause companies to miss market signals and trends. Just look at the story of Kodak. For years, this company was one of the biggest names in photography. But as digital photography began to grow in popularity, Kodak refused to adapt its business model.

Kodak took the wrong lesson from its own marketing slogan: "You press the button, we do the rest." It believed customers were more interested in the camera itself than in taking photos and sharing them digitally - so it focused on developing better cameras and declined to invest in digital imaging technologies.

As other companies developed photo-sharing platforms and smartphone cameras, Kodak lagged further and further behind in innovation. By 2012, it had filed for bankruptcy - a stark reminder that even iconic businesses can struggle if their planning isn't flexible enough to adapt to changing markets.

Blockbuster: Ignoring Streaming Video

When we think about inflexible planning, it's hard to ignore the massive failure that was Blockbuster Video. Once king of the video rental industry, Blockbuster made the mistake of completely ignoring streaming video when it came along in the late 1990s and early 2000s. This refusal to get onboard with the new technology shortly resulted in their demise.

Refusal to Adapt

With streaming services such as Netflix starting to take off, Blockbuster refused to recognize this shift in consumer preferences and simply stayed the course. When asked why they weren't investing more into streaming technology, they replied that they believed streaming was "too expensive" and only a short-term fad. But of course, this proved wrong, and Blockbuster's rigid business plan caused them to miss out on customers who wanted easier access to rental movies which eventually bankrupted them.

Lost Customers

Customers had become used to subscription-based services like Netflix that offered convenience and selection that Blockbuster just couldn't compete with - ultimately leading them down a path of closure for good. Not only did Blockbuster have too much faith in their current business plan for rental videos but also refused to invest in a new technology - arguably one of their biggest mistakes as a business.

Nokia: Refusing to Adapt to Smartphones

Once the leader in cell phones and mobile technology, Nokia's story is a classic example of what happens when an organization refuses to be flexible. In 2007, when Apple released the first iPhone and other smartphone manufacturers followed suit, Nokia believed that their existing product line (feature phones) was enough to keep them ahead of the game.

Nokia made several tactical mistakes that led to their downfall:

1. Refusing to recognize the power of smartphones.
2. Selling feature phones at too low a price.
3. Failing to develop more advanced versions of their existing products.
4. Not capitalizing on opportunities for alternatives to smartphones

By 2012, Nokia was forced to sell its handset division for $7 billion due to its inflexible stance on product pricing and not having a plan for new technology. This shows just how important it is for businesses to remain agile and adaptable in order to survive in today's fast-moving environment.

Borders: Misjudging Its Customers' Needs

Have you ever heard of Borders? It was one of the largest consumer booksellers until its bankruptcy in 2011, but - in hindsight - its failure could have been easily avoided. How so? By being more flexible with its business plan.

You see, Borders invested heavily in brick-and-mortar retail locations at a time when customers were making the switch to digital media, and that's what ended up sinking them. It was an inflexible plan that Borders stuck to even as the winds of change blew around them, leading to their downfall.

Borders failed to recognize the changing needs of its customers and had neglected to consider alternate strategies that would have allowed them to transition into their customers' new expectations. If they had been more agile and responsive during this time, they could have kept up with their customer's increasingly digital needs and potentially stayed in business.

MySpace: Overlooking Social Media Trends

When we think of outdated business plans, MySpace usually comes to mind. When it first came out in 2003, it was the first major social networking site of its kind - it allowed users to connect with their friends and family, but it also let them customize their profile pages. For a while, the site was booming and was generating a lot of revenue for its founders.

However, the company failed to keep up with the ever-changing trends in social media and were too slow to adapt to new technologies such as mobile applications. They were too focused on keeping their existing user base happy instead of recognizing the potential of new generations joining the site. As a result, they lost out on customers who preferred services like Facebook which allowed more flexibility in customization and shared content.

MySpace was unable to recover from this setback, reinforcing just how important it is for businesses to stay flexible in planning for their growth and development.

So, many popular businesses have failed because they failed to anticipate the changing market and customer needs.

This is why it's important to be open to change and to embrace flexibility in your planning process.

The key takeaway here is that it's essential to have a plan and to stick to it, but also make sure to leave room for unanticipated changes in the market that could lead to success. Don't let old methods stand in the way of innovation. Take the time to analyze all possible solutions and approaches that can help you remain competitive and solve customer problems. Be mindful of your resources, as well as the consequences of any decisions you make. In short, stay flexible in your planning to address ever-evolving customer needs and grow your business.

CHAPTER 8

Head for the Finish, Not for the Door

The Relevance of Time Management to Achieving Set Goals

Let's consider how you can improve your time management skills, including setting priorities, reducing distractions, and maximizing your productivity. Time management is one important skill that can have a significant impact on your productivity, success and overall well-being. In today's fast-paced world, it can be challenging to juggle work, family, social life, and personal development. However, mastering time management can help you achieve your goals and make the most of every moment. Time management refers to the process of organizing and planning how to allocate your time effectively to achieve desired outcomes.

Without effective time management, you may find yourself struggling to accomplish tasks, constantly feeling overwhelmed, and failing to meet deadlines. This can lead to stress, frustration, and an inability to achieve your long-term goals. By mastering time management skills, you can prioritize your tasks, increase productivity, and achieve your goals more efficiently. It allows you to make the most of your time, ensuring that you are spending it on tasks that are important and will help you achieve your desired outcomes.

Effective time management also helps to reduce stress levels by providing structure and order to your day. It allows you to plan ahead, prioritize tasks, and have a clear understanding of what needs to be accomplished each day. This can help to reduce the feeling of being overwhelmed and provide a sense of control and accomplishment. It is vital for achieving your goals. It enables you to prioritize tasks, increase productivity, reduce stress, and ultimately achieve your desired outcomes more efficiently.

There are numerous benefits to mastering effective time management. Firstly, it helps you to achieve your goals. By having a clear understanding of your priorities, you can focus your time and energy on the tasks that matter most. This ensures you make steady progress towards your objectives and are not distracted by less important tasks. Effective time management also reduces stress levels. By breaking down your tasks into manageable chunks and prioritizing them, you can avoid feeling overwhelmed and anxious. This helps you to stay calm, focused, and motivated, which ultimately leads to better results.

Another major benefit of effective time management is that it helps you to avoid procrastination. When you have a clear plan of action, you are less likely to put tasks off until the last minute or get distracted by other things. This means you can stay on track and achieve your goals more efficiently.

Effective time management can equally lead to a better work-life balance. By prioritizing your tasks and managing your time effectively, you can ensure you have time for the things that matter most to you, such as family, friends, hobbies, and relaxation. This helps to reduce stress and improve overall wellbeing, which ultimately leads to greater productivity and success in all areas of life.

Identifying your personal goals and priorities is an essential step in mastering time management. It is crucial to know what you want to achieve and what is most important to you in order to effectively manage your time and achieve your goals. Start by making a list of your short-term and long-term goals. Short-term goals are things you want to achieve within the next few days, weeks or months, while long-term goals are things you want to achieve in the future, perhaps in a year, five years or ten years from now.

Once you have your list of goals, prioritize them based on their importance to you. Think about which goals will have the biggest impact on your life and which ones you need to achieve first. This will help you focus on what is most important and avoid wasting time on things that are not aligned with your priorities.

It is equally necessary to consider your personal values and how they align with your goals. For example, if family time is important to you, then you may prioritize spending time with your loved ones over working long hours. Such a move ensures that you make decisions that are in line with your values and goals.

By identifying your personal goals and priorities, you can create a clear road map for how you spend your time and work towards achieving your goals. This will help you stay focused, motivated and on track, ultimately leading to greater success and fulfillment in your life.

Creating a daily schedule is another aspect of time management that cannot be overemphasized. Before starting your day, take some time to plan and prioritize your tasks. It helps you stay on track and focused throughout the day. Begin by making a list of all the tasks you need to complete that day. Then, prioritize them based on their importance and urgency. You can use a simple system such as the Eisenhower Matrix to help you categorize your tasks. Once you have your tasks prioritized, it's time to create a schedule. Block out time in your day for each task, making sure to allocate more time for the important and urgent tasks.

It's important to also schedule in some time for breaks and self-care. Taking breaks throughout the day can actually help you stay more productive in the long run. Use this time to stretch, take a walk, or simply give your brain a break. Be realistic with your schedule and don't over commit yourself. If you find that you're struggling to complete all your tasks, it might be time to re-evaluate your priorities or delegate some tasks to someone else.

Remember, your schedule should be a guide for your day, not a strict set of rules. Be flexible and willing to adjust as needed. By creating a daily schedule, you'll be on your way to mastering time management and achieving your goals.

The Importance of Setting Realistic Goals

Setting realistic goals is a crucial aspect of time management. Without proper goals in place, you will not know where to allocate your time, and you may end up wasting time on unimportant tasks. When setting goals, it is important to keep them realistic and achievable. Set goals that are challenging enough to keep you motivated, but not so difficult that they become overwhelming.

One way to ensure that your goals are achievable is to break them down into smaller, more manageable tasks. This can help you to stay on track and avoid feeling overwhelmed. For example, if your goal is to write a book, break it down into smaller tasks such as outlining, writing a certain number of pages each day, and editing. Another important aspect of setting realistic goals is to prioritize them. Decide which goals are most important, and focus your time and energy on those first. That ensures that you to make progress on your most important goals and avoid getting distracted by less important tasks.

It is also important to be flexible with your goals. Life can be unpredictable, and sometimes unexpected events can disrupt your plans. If this happens, don't be too hard on yourself. Instead, adjust your goals accordingly and continue to move forward.

Again, to maximize your time management skills, it is important to prioritize your tasks and delegate responsibilities wherever possible. Not all tasks are equally important or require the same amount of time and effort. Therefore, it is crucial to prioritize the tasks based on their urgency, importance, and potential impact on achieving your goals.

One effective way to prioritize tasks is to use the Eisenhower Matrix, which involves categorizing tasks into four quadrants, including urgent and important, important but not urgent, urgent but not important, and neither urgent nor important. This allows you to identify which tasks require your immediate attention and which can be deferred or delegated to others.

Delegating responsibilities is also crucial in time management. It allows you to focus on tasks that are more important and require your expertise while delegating tasks that can be handled by others. When delegating tasks, make sure to assign tasks to the right person based on their skills and knowledge. This will not only improve the quality of work but also increase efficiency and productivity.

Prioritizing tasks and delegating responsibilities are essential to optimizing your time management skills. By doing so, you can ensure that you are focusing on tasks that matter the most and maximizing your efficiency, productivity, and ultimately achieving your goals.

Optimizing the Work Environment

Your work environment plays a critical role in your productivity and overall success. If your workspace is cluttered and disorganized, it can be difficult to focus and get things done efficiently. On the other hand, a well-organized and optimized workspace can help you stay on track and minimize distractions. Here are some ways by which you can optimize your work environment:

Clean and declutter

Take some time to clean your workspace and remove any unnecessary items. It ensures you focus on your work and minimize distractions.

Set up your workspace for productivity

Make sure your desk is set up in a way that promotes productivity. Keep all the tools you need within easy reach and make sure your computer is set up for ergonomics.

Eliminate distractions

Identify any sources of distraction in your workspace and eliminate them. This could mean closing your office door, putting on noise-cancelling headphones, or turning off your phone notifications.

Add some greenery

Studies have shown that adding plants to your workspace can improve productivity and reduce stress levels. Consider adding some plants to your desk or office.

Keep it well-lit

Make sure your workspace is well-lit, as this can improve your mood and energy levels. If possible, try to get natural light into your workspace.

When you optimize your work environment, you create a space that supports your goals and helps you stay focused and productive throughout the day.

Staying motivated and focused on your goals can be challenging, especially when you have a lot on your plate. However, it's crucial to keep your eyes on the prize and stay motivated to achieve your goals. How do you achieve this?

1. Create a vision board: A vision board is a visual representation of your goals and dreams. It can help you stay motivated by reminding you of why you started in the first place.
2. Celebrate your wins: Celebrating your successes along the way can help you stay motivated and focused. Take the time to acknowledge your accomplishments and use them as fuel to keep moving forward.
3. Break down your goals: Large goals can seem overwhelming, but breaking them down into smaller, more manageable tasks can make them seem less daunting. This can help you stay focused and motivated as you work towards your larger goal.
4. Stay accountable: Find someone who can hold you accountable for your progress. This can be a friend, family member, or even a professional coach. Having someone to answer to can help keep you motivated and on track.

5. Take breaks: It's important to take breaks and recharge your batteries. Taking a short break can help you come back to your work with renewed focus and energy.

For every businessman or woman, there will be times when things aren't going according to plan, when sales are slow, or when you are facing unexpected roadblocks. It's during these times that you need to dig deep and find the motivation to keep going.

One way to stay motivated during these times is to remind yourself of your why. Why did you start this business in the first place? What is your ultimate goal? Revisiting your vision and mission statement can help remind you of your purpose and keep you on track.

Another way to stay motivated is to break your larger goals down into smaller, more manageable tasks. When you feel overwhelmed or stuck, focus on accomplishing one small task at a time. It helps you feel like you are making progress towards your larger goal, even if it's just a small step.

You also need to surround yourself with a supportive community. This can be other entrepreneurs, business coaches, or even family and friends who understand what you are going through. Having people who believe in you and support you can provide a much-needed boost when things get tough.

Remember, success is not always easy and it's not always quick. But if you stay motivated, persistent and patient, you will eventually achieve your goals. So, stay the course and keep pushing forward, even when the path ahead seems challenging.

Helpful Time Management Tools

We are living in a digital age where technology has made our lives easier. The same applies to time management. There are numerous time management tools and apps available in the market that can help you stay on track and achieve your goals. One such app is Trello, which is perfect for those who love to visualize their tasks. Trello allows you to create boards, lists, and cards to organize your tasks according to your preferences. You can also assign deadlines, add comments, and attach files to each task.

Another popular time management tool is RescueTime. It automatically tracks the time you spend on different applications and websites and provides you with detailed reports on how you spend your time. This can help you identify your time-wasting habits and improve your productivity.

If you the type that struggles with distractions, the Pomodoro Technique can be a game-changer for you. This technique involves breaking down your work into 25-minute intervals, followed by a 5-minute break. After completing four intervals, you take a longer break. There are several Pomodoro timers available online, such as Pomodoro Tracker and Focus@Will, that can help you implement this technique. However, if you prefer a more traditional approach, a simple paper planner or a bullet journal can be just as effective.

What matters is to find a tool that works for you and helps you stay on track towards achieving your goals. With the right time management tool, you can master your time and achieve your goals more efficiently.

Overcoming the "Goal Killer" - Procrastination

Procrastination is something that plagues even the best of us. It kills goals faster than a gun. It's easy to get sidetracked and lose focus, especially when you have a lot on your plate. The good news is that there are strategies that you can use to overcome procrastination and get back on track.

One of the most effective strategies is to break your goals down into smaller, more manageable tasks. When you have a large task looming over you, it can be tempting to put it off, but if you break it down into smaller steps, it becomes much more achievable. This can be done by creating a to-do list and breaking each task down into smaller, more achievable steps. Another strategy is to create a schedule and stick to it. This means setting aside specific times of the day to work on your goals and being disciplined enough to stick to that schedule. It can also be helpful to eliminate distractions, such as social media or other time-wasters, during those scheduled times.

Deal with Perfection

It is worth noting that perfectionism can often lead to procrastination. If you're constantly striving for perfection, you may find yourself putting off tasks because you're worried about not doing them perfectly. Instead, focus on doing the best you can and making progress towards your goals.

Always try to stay motivated by visualizing the end result. When you have a clear picture of what you're working towards, it can be easier to stay focused and motivated. Taking time to acknowledge your progress can be a great way to stay motivated and keep pushing forward. And don't forget to celebrate your successes along the way. But how do you track your progress?

Without knowing how far you have come, you will not be able to measure how much further you have to go. It is also important to understand that the approach you take may not always guarantee success. Therefore, you must be willing to adjust your approach as needed.

One way to track your progress is by setting milestones. These milestones should be specific, measurable, achievable, relevant, and time-bound (SMART). By breaking down your goals into smaller milestones, you can track your progress more effectively. Another way to track your progress is by keeping a daily journal or planner. You can use this to document what you accomplished each day and what you plan to work on the following day. This can help you stay focused and motivated, especially on days when you feel like you are not making progress.

Never be afraid to adjust your approach as needed. If something is not working, try a different approach. Be flexible and open to new ideas, and do not be discouraged by setbacks or failures. The most successful people are often the ones who are willing to adapt and change their approach as needed.

Mastering time management skills is necessary to achieving your goals and ultimately, success in your personal and professional life. It's important to understand that time is a finite resource and we must use it wisely. But time management is not a one-size-fits-all approach. You may need to experiment with different techniques and tools to find what works best for you. The key is to stay organized, prioritize your tasks, and eliminate distractions as much as possible.

Time management is not just about being productive all the time. It's also about taking breaks, practicing self-care, and spending time doing things you enjoy. By maintaining a healthy work-life balance, you can prevent burnout and maintain your productivity in the long run. It takes practice and commitment, but the benefits are well worth the effort. By taking control of your time, you can achieve your goals, reduce stress, and live a more fulfilling life.

Patience and Persistence for Business Success: the Winning Combination

Starting and running a business can be a challenging and sometimes daunting experience. It takes a lot of hard work, dedication, and a willingness to learn from your mistakes.

The most successful entrepreneurs, however, have discovered a winning combination that helps them overcome obstacles and achieve their goals - patience and persistence. These two traits go hand in hand and are essential for anyone who wants to succeed in business. They can help you overcome any challenges that come your way.

Why Are They Important in Business?

In achieving success in business, there are two vital ingredients that cannot be ignored – patience and persistence. The two traits are essential for entrepreneurs and business owners who want to build a thriving, sustainable business that can withstand the ups and downs of the market.

Patience is the ability to stay calm and composed in the face of challenges and setbacks, to take the long view and not get discouraged by slow progress. It's knowing that success won't happen overnight, but that with hard work and dedication, it will come eventually. Persistence, on the other hand, is the determination to keep going, to push through obstacles and keep striving even when things get tough. It's the refusal to give up or give in, to always look for ways to improve and get better. Both form a winning combination that can help entrepreneurs overcome the many obstacles that stand in the way of success.

Whether it's dealing with difficult customers, navigating a tough economic climate, or simply staying motivated in the face of adversity, these two traits can make all the difference. With both guiding your actions and decisions, you'll be well on your way to building a business that can stand the test of time.

They are often used interchangeably, but they are not the same. Patience is the ability to wait for something without getting anxious or frustrated. Persistence is the ability to keep doing something despite difficulties, obstacles, or discouragement. Patience is important in business because it takes time to build a successful business.

Patience allows the business person to wait for the right opportunities and to take calculated risks. It is important to have patience when it comes to building relationships with clients and customers. Building trust is not a quick process, and it takes time to establish a good reputation.

Persistence is equally important in business because it is what keeps a person going when things get tough. It is essential to keep pushing even when the results are not immediate. Persistent business people are tenacious and do not give up easily. They keep working towards their goals despite any setbacks they may encounter.

The key to achieving success in business is to strike a balance between patience and persistence. A person needs to be patient enough to wait for the right opportunities but persistent enough to keep working towards their goals. It is a winning combination that can lead to long-term success.

While it's important to be ambitious and driven, it's equally important to understand that success doesn't happen overnight. It takes time, effort, and often, a lot of failures along the way.

Patience is crucial because it allows you to stay focused on your goals, even when things are not going as planned. It's important to remember that every successful business has faced setbacks and challenges, but it's the entrepreneurs who remain patient and keep pushing forward who ultimately succeed.

Persistence is also crucial because it allows you to keep going even when things get tough. It's easy to give up when you face obstacles, but those who persist will eventually overcome them. Persistence also allows you to learn from your mistakes and try again, which is important in business where failure is often a necessary part of the learning process.

Developing patience and persistence is not an overnight process, but it is possible with consistent effort and dedication. How do you begin to gain these qualities?

Set Realistic Goals

Start by setting realistic goals and breaking them down into smaller achievable steps. This will help you stay focused and motivated throughout the journey.

Celebrate Small Wins

Celebrate even the smallest achievements along the way. It will help you stay encouraged and motivated as you work towards your main goal.

Learn From Setbacks

Setbacks are inevitable in any business journey, but it's important to learn from them instead of letting them discourage you. Analyze what went wrong, and how you can improve in the future.

Develop a Support System

Surround yourself with like-minded people who can provide motivation and support. Joining business groups, attending conferences, and networking events can help you build strong relationships with other entrepreneurs.

Practice Mindfulness

Practicing mindfulness techniques like meditation, deep breathing, and visualization can help you stay focused and calm during challenging times.

The Power of Delayed Gratification

Delayed gratification is an essential component of achieving long-term success in business. It is easy to get caught up in the excitement of immediate results and the desire for quick wins. However, in many cases, quick wins are not sustainable and can lead to burnout or failure in the long run. Successful business owners understand the importance of delayed gratification and the value of investing time and effort into building a strong foundation for their business. This can mean making sacrifices in the short term for greater rewards in the future.

Delayed gratification can be applied to many aspects of business, such as investing in employee training and development, building a loyal customer base, and improving product quality. These efforts may not immediately result in increased profits or growth, but they can lead to substantial benefits down the line. Delayed gratification can equally help business owners stay focused on their long-term goals and resist the temptation to chase after quick wins or short-term gains that may not align with their overall strategy. By staying patient and persistent, business owners can build a strong foundation for their business and achieve sustainable success over time.

Overcoming the Unavoidable: Obstacles and Setbacks

Obstacles and setbacks are part of any business journey. Success is not a straight line, and that setbacks are inevitable. However, setbacks can be overcome with patience and persistence. One of the keys to overcoming obstacles is to stay focused on your goals. When you encounter a setback, take the time to re-evaluate your goals and your approach. Look for ways to improve and adjust your strategy. This may involve pivoting your business model, finding new partners or collaborators, or seeking additional funding.

Another key to overcoming obstacles is to remain positive and optimistic. It's easy to get discouraged when things don't go as planned, but maintaining a positive attitude can help you stay motivated and focused on your goals. Setbacks are temporary, and with hard work and perseverance, you can overcome them. Don't be afraid to ask for help. Whether it's seeking advice from a mentor, networking with other business owners, or hiring a consultant or coach, there are many resources available to help you overcome obstacles and achieve your goals. By staying patient and persistent, and by seeking out the support and guidance you need, you can overcome any setback and achieve success in your business.

You should also understand that failure is a natural part of the journey to success. In fact, many successful entrepreneurs have experienced numerous failures before finally achieving their goals. The secret is to not let failure discourage you, but to use it as a learning opportunity and motivation to keep pushing forward. Failure is not a sign that you should give up, but a sign that you need to reassess your approach and make changes. It's important to remain persistent and patient when faced with failure in order to achieve ultimate success.

The most successful entrepreneurs are those who are able to take risks, learn from their mistakes, and continue to move forward. They understand that failure is not an ending, but a stepping stone to greater success. Failure is subjective. What may be considered a failure to one person may be considered a valuable lesson to another. It's all about your perspective and how you choose to approach the situation.

Never be afraid of failure. Embrace it, learn from it, and use it as fuel to keep pushing forward towards your goals. With patience and persistence, success is within reach for every business person. There are many examples of successful people who embody patience and persistence in their journey towards achieving their goals.

One such example is J.K. Rowling, the author of the Harry Potter series. Rowling was rejected by several publishers before finally getting her work published. She remained persistent and believed in her work, eventually becoming one of the most successful authors of all time. Another example is Jeff Bezos, the founder of Amazon. Bezos started his company in his garage and faced many challenges along the way. However, he persisted and focused on long-term goals, building Amazon into one of the most successful companies in the world.

Oprah Winfrey is also a great example of someone who embodies patience and persistence. She faced numerous obstacles in her life, including poverty and abuse, but she refused to let these challenges define her. She persisted and worked hard to achieve her goals, eventually becoming one of the most successful media moguls in history.

These individuals all share a common thread of perseverance and resilience in the face of adversity. They did not give up, even when faced with challenges and setbacks. Instead, they remained patient and persistent, believing in their vision and working tirelessly to achieve it. Their stories serve as a reminder that success is not achieved overnight, but rather through a combination of patience and persistence over time.

Patience and persistence are the very important ingredients for business success. It's important to keep in mind that success doesn't come overnight, and it's the result of consistent effort and hard work over a long period of time.

To cultivate patience and persistence, start by setting realistic goals for yourself and your business. Break them down into smaller, achievable tasks that you can tackle one by one. Celebrate small successes along the way and use them as motivation to keep going.

Setbacks and obstacles are only a natural part of life. Instead of getting discouraged, use them as opportunities to learn and grow. Stay focused on your long-term vision and don't get sidetracked by short-term setbacks. Surround yourself with a supportive community of mentors, advisors, and peers who can offer guidance and encouragement along the way. Don't be afraid to ask for help when you need it, and be open to feedback and constructive criticism.

By cultivating patience and persistence and taking actionable steps to achieve your goals, you'll be well on your way to business success. It's not always about being the fastest or the strongest, but rather about being persistent and consistent in your efforts.

Embracing Failure as a Path to Success

Everyone makes mistakes; it's simply a part of life. Some mistakes are small, while others can have a much greater impact. It's easy to feel discouraged or ashamed when we make mistakes, but what if we told you that mistakes are actually one of the best teachers you can have? By overcoming failures, you can learn valuable lessons that will ultimately lead you to success.

Failure is often seen as something negative, but in reality, it is one of the most valuable learning experiences we can have. It is through our failures that we gain insights into our strengths and vulnerabilities, allowing us to develop a more informed perspective on what we do and don't do well.

When we make mistakes or experience failures, we have the opportunity to learn from them, grow, and improve. Embracing failure as a path to success means recognizing that these setbacks are not the end of the road, but rather opportunities to learn and evolve.

Many of the most successful individuals and companies in the world have experienced major failures before achieving their success. It is through these failures that they have been able to learn, grow, and ultimately achieve their goals.

By embracing failure and learning from it, we can build resilience, develop new skills, and ultimately achieve greater success than we would have otherwise. So let's take a closer look at why mistakes are truly our best teacher and how we can use them to overcome obstacles and achieve our goals.

There is a popular saying that goes, "Failure is the mother of success." And in fact, there is scientific evidence to support this statement. Mistakes and failures are powerful tools for learning and growth. When we make mistakes, our brains are triggered to release a chemical called dopamine, which is responsible for the feeling of pleasure and reward. This chemical motivates us to seek out more of the same experience that led to its release. Essentially, our brains are wired to learn from our mistakes.

Furthermore, when we make mistakes, we are forced to analyze what went wrong and what we could have done differently. This critical reflection process helps us to develop new strategies and methods for success in the future.

In fact, some of the most successful individuals in history have attributed their success to their failures. Thomas Edison famously said, "I have not failed. I've just found 10,000 ways that won't work." Steve Jobs also spoke about the importance of failure, stating, "I didn't see it then, but it turned out that getting fired from Apple was the best thing that could have ever happened to me. It freed me to enter one of the most creative periods of my life."

So, the next time you make a mistake or experience failure, don't be discouraged. Instead, take the opportunity to learn from it and use it as a stepping stone towards ultimate success.

There are several benefits to making mistakes, and recognizing them can help you to overcome failures and achieve ultimate success. Making mistakes is a natural part of life, yet it can be difficult to accept them when they happen. However, mistakes can be the best teacher when it comes to learning and growing.

One, making mistakes can reveal areas where you need to improve. When you make a mistake, it highlights a weakness in your knowledge or skills. This presents an opportunity for growth and development. By recognizing the mistake and taking steps to correct it, you can improve and become better equipped for the future.

Secondly, making mistakes can lead to new and innovative ideas. When you encounter a problem or make a mistake, it forces you to think outside of the box and come up with creative solutions. These solutions can lead to new ideas and approaches that you may not have otherwise considered.

Again, making mistakes can build resilience and perseverance. It can be easy to become discouraged or give up after making a mistake, but failure is not the end. By learning from your mistakes and persisting through challenges, you can build resilience and perseverance, which are essential for achieving ultimate success.

Making mistakes may not be pleasant, but it can be a valuable teacher. Embracing your mistakes can lead to growth, new ideas, and increased resilience. So the next time you make a mistake, remember that it's an opportunity to learn and grow, and it's a necessary part of the journey towards success.

Fears Hold You Back from Embracing Failure

Fear of failure is one of the most common fears that people face. Many individuals hold themselves back from trying new things or taking risks because they're afraid of making mistakes or failing. This fear can be so overwhelming that it prevents people from even attempting to pursue their dreams or goals.

One other common fear that holds people back is the fear of what others will think. People often worry that if they fail, they'll be judged, ridiculed or even rejected by others. This fear of being judged can be so intense that it can stop people from even trying, let alone succeeding.

There's also the fear of the unknown. People are often afraid of what they don't know or understand, and this can hold them back from taking action or trying new things.

The fear of losing control can also be a major roadblock to embracing failure. People often feel like they need to be in control of everything and when they face a situation where failure is a possibility, they feel like they are losing control.

It's essential to recognize these fears and understand that they are normal human emotions. The key to overcoming these fears is to face them head-on and understand that failure is a natural part of the learning and growth process. By pushing through these fears and embracing failure, you'll become more resilient, more confident and ultimately more successful.

One of the most important things to bear in mind when coping with failure is to not let it define you. Failure is a natural part of the learning process, and it's how you respond to it that determines your ultimate success. It's important to acknowledge your mistakes, learn from them, and move forward with the lessons you've learned. One way to cope with failure is to reframe it as a learning opportunity. Take the time to reflect on what went wrong, why it happened, and what you can do differently next time. Such will help you identify areas for growth and improvement, and will ultimately help you become more resilient in the face of future challenges.

Another important aspect of coping with failure is to have a growth mindset. This means embracing challenges, seeing them as opportunities for growth, and believing that your abilities can be developed through hard work and dedication. This mindset will help you stay focused on your goals, and will help you persevere in the face of setbacks.

Surround yourself with a supportive network of friends, family, and colleagues who can provide encouragement, advice, and perspective during difficult times. Having a support system can help you stay motivated, keep things in perspective, and remind you of the progress you've made along the way. Failure is not the end of the world. It's an opportunity to learn, grow, and ultimately succeed in ways you never thought possible. By adopting the right mindset and coping strategies, you can turn your failures into your greatest success stories.

The Power of a Growth Mindset

The power of a growth mindset is immeasurable when it comes to overcoming failures for ultimate success. A growth mindset is the belief that you can develop and improve your skills, knowledge, and abilities through hard work, dedication, and perseverance. In other words, it's the belief that you can learn from your mistakes and failures and use them as a tool to grow and develop.

People with a growth mindset view failures as opportunities for growth and learning. They don't give up easily, and they don't let setbacks define them. Instead, they use their failures as a catalyst for success. They analyze their mistakes, identify what went wrong, and use that information to make improvements and better decisions moving forward.

Having a growth mindset is particularly important when it comes to entrepreneurship and business. Starting a business is not easy, and setbacks and failures are inevitable. But if you have a growth mindset, you can use those setbacks and failures as a tool to learn, grow, and eventually succeed. So, if you want to overcome failures and achieve ultimate success, it's important to cultivate a growth mindset. Embrace challenges, view failures as opportunities, and focus on continuous learning and growth. With a growth mindset, you'll be better equipped to overcome obstacles and achieve the success you desire.

Strategies for Learning from Mistakes and Moving Forward

Learning from mistakes is critical in achieving ultimate success. However, it's not always easy to face our mistakes and move on from them. Let me highlight some strategies that will help you learn from your mistakes and continue moving forward:

1. Own your mistake: Acknowledging that you made a mistake is the first step in learning from it. Take responsibility for your actions and don't make excuses.
2. Analyze what went wrong: Reflect on what caused the mistake and what you could have done differently. It ensures that you avoid making the same mistake in the future.
3. Learn from others: Seek advice and guidance from others who have experienced similar mistakes. This will give you a new perspective and provide you with valuable insights.
4. Focus on the solution: Instead of dwelling on the mistake, focus on finding a solution to the

problem. It will help you move forward and prevent the mistake from happening again.
5. Embrace failure: Failure is a natural part of the learning process. Embrace it and use it as a tool to help you grow and develop.

It's not always easy to bounce back from setbacks. That's why it's important to have tools and strategies in place to help you overcome mistakes and achieve your goals.

One tool that can help is self-reflection. Take some time to reflect on what went wrong and what you can do differently next time. This can help you identify patterns and avoid making the same mistakes in the future. It's important to approach self-reflection with a growth mindset, rather than beating yourself up over the mistake.

Seeking feedback from others is another tool for overcoming mistakes. This can be from a mentor, colleague, or friend. Hearing different perspectives and ideas can help you gain new insights and approaches to problems.

Goal-setting is one other way for achieving success. By setting clear and measurable goals, you can identify what steps you need to take to reach your desired outcome. It's important to break down your goals into smaller, actionable steps to make them more achievable.

It is also necessary to stay resilient when faced with setbacks. Resilience is the ability to withstand and recover from difficult situations. It's an essential trait that separates those who give up after a setback from those who push through and come out stronger on the other side. Don't let one setback derail your progress. Building resilience is not an overnight process, but it's worth the effort to develop this important skill.

To build resilience is to practice self-compassion. When you experience a setback, it's easy to be hard on yourself and spiral into negative self-talk. Instead, remind yourself that mistakes are a natural part of the learning process, and be kind and understanding towards yourself.

Another important factor in building resilience is having a support system. Surround yourself with people who believe in you and support you, and seek out their guidance and encouragement when you're feeling defeated. Additionally, try to find a mentor or coach who can offer you objective feedback and help you stay focused on your goals.

One other powerful way to build resilience is to embrace challenges and failures as opportunities for growth. Instead of avoiding difficult situations or beating yourself up when things don't go as planned, look for the lessons and opportunities for improvement. By reframing setbacks in this way, you can turn them into valuable learning experiences and emerge even stronger and more resilient than before.

Understand that failure is not the end. In fact, it's often the beginning of a new journey that can lead to ultimate success. Mistakes and failures are simply lessons that we can learn from to improve ourselves and our strategies going forward. That's why it's crucial to embrace failure and use it as a tool for growth and development.

As we have discussed throughout this book, the secret to overcoming failure is to maintain a positive mindset and use these experiences as opportunities to learn, pivot and improve. By doing so, you can develop resilience and drive that will serve you well in all aspects of your life. Success is not a straight line. It is often the result of countless failures and mistakes that have taught us valuable lessons along the way. So don't be afraid to take risks, embrace your failures and use them as a stepping stone towards your ultimate success.

CHAPTER 9

Why Don't You Get a Job?

Before You Get That Job

We all have that one friend who is stuck in a job they hate but can't seem to break free. Perhaps you're that friend. The truth is, settling for a stagnant career can be a costly decision. Staying in a job you don't enjoy or doesn't pay all your bills can lead to frustration, boredom, and burnout. It can also lead to a lack of motivation and a loss of passion for your work. Not only can this negatively impact your mental health, but it can also affect your physical well-being. The cost of a stagnant career goes beyond just how it makes you feel, it can impact your financial future as well. So, be careful. You may want to consider investing just your money in someone else's business and just live on dividends if setting out every day to work doesn't pay you.

Now let's examine why some people settle for less in their careers.

Many people settle for less in their careers because they feel stuck or trapped. They may have a job that pays the bills but doesn't challenge them or provide opportunities for growth. Others may be afraid to take risks or try something new, so they stay in a job that feels comfortable and familiar. Fear is a major factor that keeps people from pursuing their dreams and taking risks. Fear of failure, fear of the unknown, and fear of change are all common reasons why people settle for less in their careers. They may feel that they lack the skills or experience needed to pursue a different career path or they may worry about the financial implications of making a change.

Again, a reason why people settle for less in their careers is that they may not be aware of their options. They may not know what other career paths are available to them or they may not know how to go about pursuing a new career. Lack of information and guidance can be a major barrier to career growth and development.

So, people settle for less in their careers due to fear, lack of information, and feeling stuck. Settling for less can have a high cost in terms of job satisfaction, career growth, and financial stability.

I will advise you to take risks, pursue your passions, and seek out new opportunities to ensure a fulfilling and successful career. Stagnation in your career can be detrimental in more ways than one. It can lead to a lack of job satisfaction and motivation, which can make you unhappy and unfulfilled in your work life. This can spill over into your personal life as well, affecting your relationships and overall well-being.

Again, a stagnant career can also have a significant impact on your financial situation. Without opportunities for advancement or growth, you may find yourself stuck in a lower paying job or with limited earning potential. This can make it difficult to save for the future, pay off debts, or even cover day-to-day expenses.

In addition to these personal costs, a stagnant career can also have a negative impact on your professional reputation. If you are not seen as someone who is willing to learn, grow, and take on new challenges, you may be overlooked for promotions or opportunities. This can limit your ability to build a network of professional contacts and could make it harder to find new job opportunities in the future.

Settling for a stagnant career can have far-reaching consequences. It's important to take control of your professional development and seek out opportunities for growth and advancement in order to avoid the high cost of settling for less.

The Effects of Staying in a Job That Does Not Satisfy You

Settling for a job you do not enjoy or have passion for may seem like the easy or safe choice in the short term, but the long-term consequences can be severe. It's important to prioritize your health, happiness, and career growth by taking steps to find a job that you love and that challenges and fulfills you.

Staying in a job that doesn't give you joy anymore can have serious negative effects on your physical and mental health. It can lead to depression, anxiety, stress, and even physical health problems like high blood pressure and heart disease. These negative effects can spill over into other areas of your life, such as your personal relationships and your overall sense of well being. It can also limit your career growth and earning potential. If you find yourself feeling stuck in your current position with few opportunities for advancement or salary increases, leave. This is because it can lead to feelings of frustration, resentment, and even anger towards your employer.

Then again, it can hold you back from pursuing your true passions and interests. You may find yourself feeling unfulfilled and unhappy with your career, which can lead to a sense of regret later in life.

How a Stagnant Career Affects Personal Life

Career occupies a noble place in anyone's life, and it can have a significant impact on your personal life. When you settle for less and become stagnant in your career, it can have several negative effects on your personal life. It can lead to a lack of motivation and enthusiasm. You may start to feel unfulfilled, frustrated, and dissatisfied with your work, which can often spill over into your personal life. You may become disengaged, irritable, and negative, which can affect your relationships with friends, family, and loved ones.

It can also have financial implications. If you're not growing in your career and earning a higher income, you may struggle to meet your financial needs and achieve your goals. This can cause stress and tension in your personal life, leading to anxiety and other mental health problems.

A stagnant career can limit your personal growth and development too. You may feel stuck in a rut, with limited opportunities for learning and advancement. This can hinder your personal growth and make you feel like you're not living up to your potential.

How a Stagnant Career Affects Your Financial stability

A stagnant career can have a huge impact on your financial stability. When you remain in the same position for too long, your salary may not increase as much as it would if you were to switch jobs or climb the career ladder within your organization.

Staying in the same role for an extended period of time can also make you feel undervalued and unchallenged which can lead to a lack of motivation and productivity. This, in turn, can affect your performance which may lead to missed opportunities for promotions or salary increments. Over time, this lack of financial growth can have a significant impact on your overall wealth and financial stability. If you're not earning enough to cover your expenses, it can lead to debt and financial stress which can have a negative impact on your mental and physical health.

Moreover, if you're not earning enough to save for your retirement or other financial goals, you may find yourself struggling in the long term. It's important to assess your financial situation regularly and take proactive steps to improve it. This may include seeking out new job opportunities, pursuing additional education or training, or developing new skills to make yourself more marketable in your industry. By taking these steps, you can prevent the negative impact of a stagnant career on your financial stability and secure your financial future.

Does it have any impact on your professional development?

Settling for a stagnant career could have a detrimental impact on your professional development in the long run. When you stay in the same role or company for an extended period of time, it could lead to a lack of growth opportunities, resulting in a lack of new skills and experiences. This can lead to professional stagnation, which can make it difficult to advance in your career or even stay relevant in your industry.

Also, if you are not continuously learning new skills and gaining new experiences, your value as an employee may decrease over time. This means that you may not be considered for high-level positions, promotions or even new job opportunities.

In today's fast-paced world, industries are constantly evolving, and new technologies and practices are emerging all the time.

It's crucial for professionals to keep up with the latest trends and developments to remain competitive in the job market.

By settling for less, you could be limiting your potential for growth and development, which could result in a stagnant career and limited opportunities for professional advancement.

Leaving a stagnant career can be scary, but taking the steps to move towards a more fulfilling future can be incredibly rewarding. Don't settle for less, take control of your career and work towards the life you want to lead.

So, if you're feeling stuck in a job, how do you break out of this stronghold to take control of your career and start taking steps towards a more fulfilling future?

Identify your goals

It's important to have a clear idea of what you want to achieve in your career. Start by identifying your interests, skills, and passions. That narrows down your options and identify career paths that are most suitable for you. Write down your objectives and be specific about what you want to achieve.

Research

Once you have identified your passion, do your due diligence and research the industry or job you want to move into. This will help you to understand the skills, experience and qualifications you need to acquire at the time. Make sure to research the job market and employment trends in your chosen field.

Upskill

Depending on your career goals, you may need to get additional training or education. This could be in the form of a certification, diploma, or degree program. Once you know what you need to learn, start acquiring those skills. You can do this by taking courses, attending workshops, or networking with people in such a field.

Network

Networking is a great way to learn more about your chosen career, gain insights from professionals in the field, and develop relationships that could lead to job opportunities. Building relationships with people in your desired field can help you to gain insights, advice, and even job opportunities. Attend industry events, join relevant groups on social media, and reach out to people on LinkedIn.

Be patient

Changing careers can take time, so be patient with yourself. Don't expect to land your dream job overnight, but keep working towards it and stay focused on your goals. You may have to start at the bottom and work your way up, but with dedication and hard work, you can achieve your career goals.

Making a career change is not an easy decision, but it can be one of the most rewarding choices you will ever make. With the right mindset, preparation, and support, you can successfully transition to a new career and achieve your professional goals.

So why is it better to work where your passion is?

Pursuing your dreams and passions can be one of the most rewarding experiences of your life. It can lead to immense personal growth, greater fulfillment, and a deep sense of purpose. When you are passionate about something, it drives you to work harder, learn more, and push yourself further than you ever thought possible. This kind of drive and motivation can result in significant achievements, both personally and professionally.

When you are doing something you love, it doesn't feel like work. Instead, it feels like a natural extension of who you are. This can lead to greater job satisfaction, increased productivity, and a better overall quality of life. Pursuing your passions can also lead to opportunities you never thought possible. Whether it's starting your own business, working with like-minded individuals, or traveling the world, the possibilities are endless.

Moreover, the rewards of pursuing your passions are not just limited to personal gratification. This kind of pursuit also brings immense value to the world. When you are working on something you are truly passionate about, you are likely to create something of great value that can benefit others. Whether it's a new product, a service, or a piece of art, your passion and dedication can lead to creations that have the power to change lives and inspire others.

Therefore, pursuing your dreams and passions can be a deeply rewarding experience that brings immense personal and professional benefits. Don't settle for less and always strive towards what truly drives and fulfills you.

Why You should Consider Owning a Business

Would it be wrong to say that everyone's dream is to be their own boss? Won't you love to set your own hours, being in charge of your own business, and reaping the rewards of your hard work?

More and more people are realizing the benefits of owning their own business, rather than being employed by someone else. While it can be a challenging and sometimes daunting road, there are many reasons why being your own boss is worth it. From having greater control over your career and financial stability, to experiencing a greater sense of personal fulfillment, owning your own business offers a range of rewards that simply can't be matched by working for someone else.

It could be that you are looking for more freedom and flexibility in your work schedule, or perhaps you're ready to take charge of your own financial future, but your 9-5 job is getting in the way. Whatever the reason, owning a business can be a great way to achieve these goals and more. Some people really don't understand this - they simply leave one 9-5 job and move to another which at first often seem better. With time, they get frustrated again. How do you end this? Become your own boss.

From the ability to set your own schedule, to the potential for unlimited income, to the satisfaction of building something from the ground up, there are many reasons why entrepreneurship can be a fulfilling and rewarding path.

So, whether you're considering starting your own business or you're already a business owner looking for inspiration, you will discover the reason why it pays to put your efforts in what belongs to you.

When I and my family immigrated to Australia in 2013, we had just four suitcases with our cloths that was it, first I had a cleaning job after that I started a food company and later a restaurant as well. After a heart attack in 2018 I decided to go into a slower mode because of my health condition and turned into the investment side of doing business. As you do nobody sees you "Working". And as many presume: if you do not leave your house at 6am to return at 6pm, you must be unemployed.

This question will often arise at some point: "Why don't you get a job?" People will just be worried about your sitting at home. They would always expect to see you walk briskly to the office every morning. No one cares whether are actually satisfied with the job. It is near to impossible to explain to people who value a "safe and secure" job why it can be better to not have a job.

For example, the income you generate from a job is fixed - it has a "Glass ceiling". As you go along, you cannot make more hours in a day. However, if you own a business, your opportunities are "unlimited". You don't have to be actively involved - you can employ competent hands to run the business on your behalf or simply outsource the work. With a job, you have no freedom than that what the boss allows you. But when you are the boss, you decide when and when not to do anything.

Now look at the many benefits of running a business, especially one within the confines of your passion:

Flexibility and Work-Life Balance

One of the biggest benefits of being your own boss is the flexibility and work-life balance that comes with owning a business. As an employee, you may be required to work set hours, take minimal breaks, and have limited vacation days. However, when you own a business, you have the freedom to set your own schedule and work around your personal life.

Many entrepreneurs have the flexibility to work from home, which is a huge advantage in today's digital age. This allows for more time with family, less time spent commuting, and a better work-life balance overall. It also allows for the ability to work during hours that are most productive for you, whether that means working early in the morning or late at night.

Additionally, owning a business allows for more control over the workload. You have the ability to delegate tasks and responsibilities as needed, which can help to alleviate stress and create a more manageable workload. As an employee, you may be given tasks that are outside of your expertise or skillset, which can be frustrating and overwhelming. As a business owner, you have the opportunity to hire employees or contract out work to professionals who have the necessary skills and experience. The flexibility and work-life balance that comes with owning a business can lead to a more fulfilling and enjoyable career. It allows for more time with loved ones, the ability to work when you are most productive, and the opportunity to create a more balanced lifestyle.

Unlimited Income Potential

One of the major benefits of being your own boss is the ability to earn unlimited income. When working for someone else, you are usually paid a set salary or hourly wage, which limits your earning potential. However, when you own your own business, your income potential is unlimited.

As a business owner, your income is directly tied to the success of your business. If you work hard, make smart decisions, and grow your business, your income will increase accordingly. This means that you have the ability to earn as much money as you want, without being limited by a salary cap or pay grade.

Furthermore, owning a business allows you to create multiple streams of income. You can diversify your revenue streams by offering new products or services, expanding into new markets, or creating passive income streams, such as affiliate marketing or selling digital products.

Of course, building a successful business takes time, effort, and dedication. But the potential rewards are worth it. With unlimited income potential, you have the ability to achieve financial freedom, build wealth, and create the life you've always wanted.

Freedom to Pursue Passion Projects

One of the most significant benefits of owning a business is the freedom to pursue passion projects. When you work for someone else, you are often limited to doing tasks and projects that are assigned to you. You may not have the opportunity to explore your own interests and passions in your work.

However, when you own your own business, you have the freedom to pursue projects that align with your passions and interests. This can be incredibly fulfilling and motivating. It also allows you to bring your unique skills and perspectives to your business, which can help it stand out from competitors.

For example, if you own a bakery and have a passion for creating unique and innovative dessert recipes, you can experiment and create new products that reflect this passion. This can help your bakery stand out from other bakeries in your area and attract customers who are interested in trying new and exciting desserts.

Pursuing passion projects can also help you stay motivated and engaged in your work. When you are doing work that you are passionate about, it doesn't feel like work at all. It becomes something you enjoy doing and look forward to each day.

In summary, owning a business gives you the freedom to pursue passion projects, which can be incredibly fulfilling and motivating. It can also help your business stand out from competitors and attract customers who are interested in what you have to offer.

Control Over Business Decisions

A great benefit of being your own boss is having complete control over business decisions. When you're employed by someone else, you'll need to follow their vision and make decisions based on their priorities. This can be frustrating if you have your own ideas about how things should be done. But as a business owner, you have complete autonomy to make decisions that affect the direction and success of your business. This can be liberating and empowering, as you are not reliant on others to make decisions that will impact your livelihood.

Having control over business decisions also allows you to be more agile and responsive to changes in the market. You can pivot your business strategy quickly if it's not working or take advantage of new opportunities as they arise. Moreover, as a business owner, you get to choose the people you work with and the culture you want to create in your business. This means you can hire employees that share your values and vision, creating a positive and productive work environment.

Therefore, having control over business decisions offers a level of freedom and creativity that is difficult to attain when working for someone else. It's one of the biggest draws of entrepreneurship and can lead to a more fulfilling and rewarding career.

Sense of Accomplishment

Being your own boss has a sense of accomplishment that comes with it. When you're an employee, you may have specific tasks and goals to accomplish, but ultimately, you're working to achieve someone else's vision. When you're the owner of a business, every success is your own. You have the freedom to set your own goals and work towards achieving them on your own terms.

The sense of accomplishment that comes with owning a business is hard to beat. Whether it's hitting revenue targets, reaching a new customer base, or launching a new product, each step towards your goals can be incredibly rewarding. As a business owner, you have the autonomy to make decisions and execute them, and that feeling of control can be incredibly empowering.

Also, owning a business also provides the opportunity to create a legacy. Building something from scratch and seeing it grow and succeed is an incredible feeling that can leave a lasting impact on both you and your community. Whether you're creating jobs, contributing to the local economy, or simply providing a valuable service to your customers, the sense of accomplishment that comes with owning a business is truly unparalleled.

Opportunities for Personal and Professional Growth

We may say the most rewarding aspects of being your own boss is the opportunity for personal and professional growth. When you own a business, you are responsible for everything from the finances to the marketing to the day-to-day operations. This means that you have to constantly be learning and improving in order to keep your business running smoothly.

In addition to the skills you learn on the job, owning a business also presents ample opportunities for personal growth. You will be forced to step outside of your comfort zone and take on new challenges, whether it's networking with potential clients, pitching your business to investors, or managing a team of employees. These experiences will help you develop a sense of confidence and self-assuredness that can be difficult to cultivate in a traditional employment setting.

An additional benefit of being your own boss is the ability to set your own goals and pursue your passions. When you work for someone else, you are often limited by their vision and goals for the company. However, as a business owner, you have the freedom to set your own priorities and pursue the projects and initiatives that interest you the most.

Owning that business may be a challenging but it is an incredibly rewarding experience that can lead to both personal and professional growth. If you are someone who is passionate about your work and eager to take on new challenges, then starting your own business may be the perfect career path for you.

Tax Benefits of Being a Business Owner

Another advantage of owning a business is the tax benefits that come with it. As a business owner, you can legally write off a number of expenses that you otherwise would not be able to if you were an employee working for someone else. For example, you can write off expenses such as office rent, utilities, equipment, and even your own health insurance premiums. You can also claim deductions for expenses such as business travel, meals, and entertainment.

Besides, owning a business can help you save money on taxes. As a business owner, you can take advantage of tax planning strategies to minimize your tax bill. For instance, you can set up a retirement plan for yourself and your employees, which can help you reduce your taxable income.

In addition, you can also take advantage of tax-deferred savings plans such as a SEP-IRA, which allows you to contribute up to 25% of your net self-employment income, up to a maximum of $58,000 per year. This can help you save a significant amount of money on taxes while also providing for your retirement.

The tax benefits of owning a business can be very attractive, and they can help you keep more of your hard-earned money in your pocket.

Building a Legacy for Future Generations

Building a legacy for future generations is one of the most rewarding aspects of owning a business. When you're your own boss, you have the unique opportunity to build something that can last beyond your lifetime, providing financial security and stability for your family and future generations. By creating a successful business from scratch, you are also creating a valuable asset that can be passed down through generations, providing a sense of pride and accomplishment for your family.

As your business grows, you have the opportunity to create employment opportunities for others, which can have a positive impact on your local economy. This is especially important in today's world, where many people are struggling to find work due to the economic downturn caused by the pandemic.

Owning a business also allows you to give back to your community by supporting local charities and organizations. By doing so, you're not only contributing to the betterment of those around you but also building a strong reputation for your business. All of these factors contribute to building a legacy that goes beyond just financial success. Owning a successful business can be a source of pride for you and your family, and a way to make a lasting impact on your community and society as a whole.

Now that you have understood the benefits, waste no time anymore! Take actions. Before you get that job you are considering, ask yourself these questions:

1. Is my job safe and secure?
2. I'm I happy in this role?
3. Do I use my full talents in this role?
4. How much can I make to lift my family standard of living?
5. How free am I going to go on a vacation or have a day off work?

If your candid answers to all of these questions are not satisfactory, the right way to go is business! Find your passion and turn it into a venture.

Yes, owning a business can be a lot of work, but the rewards are numerous. It can provide you with the freedom and flexibility to create your own schedule, follow your passions, and build a legacy for yourself. While it's not for everyone, owning a business can be an incredibly fulfilling experience if you're willing to put in the work.

Chapter 10

Get a Mentor

The Power of Mentorship: Why You Need a Mentor to Grow Your Business

Success is never easy, but with the right guidance, it can be achieved more efficiently. One of the most powerful tools available to entrepreneurs and business owners is mentorship. A mentor is an experienced and trusted advisor who can offer guidance, support, and encouragement to help you reach your goals.

A business mentor can provide invaluable insights into your industry, help you avoid common pitfalls, and provide advice on navigating business challenges. In this post, we will explore the power of mentorship and how it can help boost your success. Whether you are an entrepreneur just starting out or a seasoned business owner looking to take your company to the next level, a business mentor can be a significant factor in your success story.

What Is Mentorship and Why Is It Important?

Mentorship is a relationship between a more experienced and knowledgeable person (the mentor) and a less experienced person (the mentee) in which the mentor provides guidance, advice, and support to the mentee. In the business world, mentorship has become increasingly important in recent years as entrepreneurs and professionals seek to gain an edge in their respective fields.

One of the primary benefits of mentorship is the ability to learn from someone who has already achieved success in your desired area. A good mentor can provide invaluable insights into the industry, offer advice on how to navigate challenges and obstacles, and provide a sounding board for ideas and strategies.

Mentorship can also help to accelerate your learning curve and avoid common mistakes. By having a mentor who has already experienced the ups and downs of starting and growing a business, you can benefit from their knowledge and expertise without having to learn everything through trial and error.

Working with a mentor can provide a sense of accountability and motivation. Knowing that you have someone who is invested in your success and is there to support you can be a powerful motivator to push through challenges and pursue your goals. Mentorship is a powerful tool for anyone looking to achieve success in their business or career. By working with a mentor, you can gain valuable knowledge and insights, avoid common mistakes, and stay motivated and accountable as you work towards your goals.

Having a business mentor can be an invaluable asset in achieving success since a mentor is someone who has been where you are and has succeeded in the industry you are trying to break into. He or she can provide guidance, advice, and support to help you navigate the challenges and obstacles that come with building a successful business. A major benefit of having a mentor is the ability to learn from their experiences. They can share their insights and knowledge, providing you with a roadmap to success. They can help you identify blind spots in your business and provide feedback that can help you improve your strategies and tactics.

In addition to providing advice and guidance, a mentor can also help you expand your network. As an established professional in your industry, your mentor likely has a vast network of contacts that they can introduce you to. This can help you build relationships and partnerships that can be instrumental in growing your business.

Having a mentor can help you stay accountable. When you set goals for yourself and your business, your mentor can check in with you regularly to make sure you are staying on track. This can be a powerful motivator, helping you stay focused and committed to achieving success.

But locating the right business mentor is more crucial to your success. It's important to work with someone who has the experience and skills that you need to develop in order to achieve your goals. A good mentor will help you to identify your strengths and weaknesses, and will guide you in developing the skills you need to succeed in your industry.

It's also important to find a mentor who shares your values and goals. A mentor who is aligned with your values and goals will be much more effective at helping you to achieve your objectives than someone who doesn't. Look for someone who has experience in your industry, and who has a track record of success.

Availability is one other important factor to consider when finding a mentor. Make sure that your mentor has enough time to commit to your development, and that they are accessible when you need them. A good mentor should be able to provide you with regular feedback and support, as well as help you to identify new opportunities for growth and development.

Finding the right mentor is not a one-size-fits-all process. Take the time to identify your own personal goals and values, and seek out someone who can help you to achieve them.

Types of Mentorship

Mentorship comes in all shapes and sizes, and it's important to choose the type of mentorship that best suits your needs and goals. There are several types of mentorship available, including:

Formal Mentorship

This type of mentorship is typically structured and organized. It often involves a program where mentees are paired with experienced mentors who provide guidance and support over a set period of time.

Informal Mentorship

This type of mentorship is less structured and often happens naturally. It involves approaching someone who is experienced in your field and asking for their guidance and advice.

Peer Mentorship

This type of mentorship involves partnering with someone who is at a similar career stage as you. You can support and learn from each other as you progress through your careers.

Virtual Mentorship

This type of mentorship is conducted online, often through video conferencing or email. It allows you to connect with mentors who are not geographically close to you.

The type of mentorship that is best for you depends on your needs and goals. If you're looking for a more structured and formal approach, you may want to consider a formal mentorship program. If you prefer a more casual approach, informal or peer mentorship may be a better fit. Virtual mentorship is a great option if you're looking to connect with mentors who are not in your immediate area.

Whichever type of mentorship you choose, the relationship should be mutually beneficial. Both parties should be learning and growing from the experience. It is only then you can gain valuable insights and guidance that will help you achieve your goals and boost your success.

Steps to Finding the Right Mentor

It can be a daunting task to find the perfect mentor, but it's an important step towards achieving success in your business. Here are some tips to help you find the right mentor:

1. Identify your needs: Before you start your search for a mentor, identify your needs and goals. What specific areas of your business do you need help with? What skills do you want to develop? It will help you narrow down your search and find a mentor who aligns with your goals.
2. Look within your network: Start by looking within your existing network. Do you know anyone who has experience in your industry or has achieved success in a similar business? Reach out to them and ask if they would be willing to mentor you.
3. Join a mentorship program: Many organizations offer mentorship programs for entrepreneurs. These programs match you with a mentor who has experience in your industry and can provide guidance and support.
4. Attend networking events: Attend networking events and conferences in your industry to meet potential mentors. This is a great way to expand your network and build relationships with other entrepreneurs.
5. Be open and receptive: Once you've found a potential mentor, be open and receptive to their advice and guidance. Be honest about your weaknesses and areas where you need help, and be willing to take their feedback and implement changes in your business.

Note that getting a mentor for your business is not a one-time event. It's an ongoing process of building relationships and seeking guidance to help you achieve success in your business. With the right mentor by your side, you can accelerate your growth and achieve your goals faster than you ever thought possible. You'll be able to achieve more than you ever thought possible. Mentors can provide you access to their network. Mentors often have established connections and relationships with other professionals and industry leaders that can be valuable to your own business. They can introduce you to potential partners, clients, or investors, and help you expand your own network.

Having a mentor can also boost your confidence and motivation. Starting and running a business can be a lonely and challenging experience, and having a mentor who believes in you and your ideas can make all the difference in keeping you motivated and focused on your goals. Having a business mentor can be a transformative experience for your business, providing you with the support, knowledge, and connections you need to succeed.

What to Expect from Your Business Mentor

Your business mentor should be someone who is experienced and knowledgeable in your field of business. They should have a track record of success and have faced similar challenges to what you are currently experiencing. Your mentor should be someone you trust and are comfortable talking to about your business goals and struggles.

When you first start working with your mentor, you should set clear expectations and goals for what you hope to achieve through the mentorship. Discuss the frequency and mode of communication that will work best for both of you. It's important to also establish boundaries and understand the limitations of your mentor's time and availability.

During your mentorship, you should expect to receive honest and constructive feedback, guidance on decision-making, and support in setting and achieving goals. Your mentor should be someone who challenges you to think critically and creatively about your business while also providing a safe and supportive environment to discuss challenges and failures.

Never forget that mentorship is a two-way street. You should also be willing to put in the work and listen to your mentor's advice. Be open to feedback and willing to make changes to your business strategies when necessary. With the right mentor, you can gain valuable insights, avoid common pitfalls, and achieve greater success in your business.

Building a successful relationship with your mentor is necessary for both parties to reap the benefits of mentorship. How do you achieve this?

1. Be clear about your goals: Clearly communicate your goals and what you hope to achieve through the mentorship. This will help your mentor tailor their advice and support to your specific needs.
2. Be respectful of their time: Remember that your mentor is likely a busy professional with their own commitments. Be respectful of their time and make sure that you are prepared for each meeting with an agenda and specific questions or topics you would like to discuss.
3. Be open and honest: Honesty is essential to any successful relationship, and mentorship is no exception. Be open and honest about your challenges, successes, and areas where you need support. This will help your mentor provide you with the best possible guidance and advice.
4. Act on their advice: Your mentor is providing you with valuable guidance and advice based on their own experiences. It's important to be receptive to their advice and take action on it. Let them know how you have implemented their advice and the impact it has had on your business or career.
5. Show gratitude: Mentorship is a two-way street, and it's important to show your mentor that you appreciate their time and support. A simple thank you note or small token of appreciation can go a long way in building a successful relationship with your mentor.

By following these tips, you can build a successful relationship with your mentor and take full advantage of the power of mentorship to boost your success.

How Do You Incorporate Mentorship into Your Overall Business Strategy?

Incorporating mentorship into your overall business strategy can help you in a variety of ways. It can help you gain valuable insights from someone who has already gone through the journey you are currently on. They can provide you with guidance, advice, and knowledge that can help you make better decisions, avoid common pitfalls, and accelerate your growth.

To incorporate mentorship into your business strategy, start by identifying areas where you need support. Do you lack experience in a certain area of business, such as marketing or finance? Or are you struggling with a particular challenge, like scaling your business or managing your time?

Once you have identified these areas, look for mentors who have experience in those areas. There are many ways to find a mentor, from LinkedIn and industry events to business associations and networking groups. You can also consider joining a formal mentorship program or hiring a business coach. Once you have found a mentor, be clear about your goals and expectations, and establish a regular schedule for meetings or calls.

Recall I said that mentorship is a two-way street. It's not just about what you can gain from your mentor, but also what you can offer in return. Be willing to share your own knowledge and insights, and be open to feedback and constructive criticism. With the right mentor, you can take your business to the next level and achieve greater success than you ever thought possible.

Key Takeaways for Entrepreneurs Seeking Business Mentors

If you're an entrepreneur seeking a business mentor, here are some key takeaways to keep in mind.

First, it's important to find someone who has experience in your industry or a related industry. It ensures that they have a good understanding of the challenges you face and can provide valuable insights and guidance.

Second, look for a mentor who has a track record of success. This doesn't necessarily mean that they've never experienced failure, but rather that they've learned from their mistakes and have a proven ability to overcome obstacles.

Next, be willing to be open and honest with your mentor. A good mentor will challenge you to think differently and consider new approaches to your business, but they can only do this if you're willing to be vulnerable and share your thoughts and ideas.

Furthermore, set clear goals and expectations for the mentorship relationship. This will help ensure that both you and your mentor are on the same page about what you hope to achieve and how you will work together to get there.

Lastly, a business mentor is just one part of your support system. It's important to also seek out other resources, such as networking groups, industry associations, and business coaches, to help you achieve your goals and grow your business.

Collaboration over Competition: Growing Your Business Through Idea Exchange with Niche Partners.

An alternative to mentorship is partnership - partnership with players in your niche but not necessarily in your product line.

In today's competitive business landscape, it can be tempting to view other businesses within your niche as rivals or even enemies. However, this mindset can be counterproductive and limit your growth potential. By embracing collaboration over competition, you can build strong relationships with niche partners and leverage their expertise and audience to grow your own business.

Let us discuss the benefits of partnering with other businesses in your niche and how idea exchange can help you reach new customers and expand your offerings.

I will also show you how to identify potential partners, establish trust, and create win-win collaborations that benefit everyone involved. So if you're ready to take your business to the next level, read on.

Collaboration is a significant factor in growing any business. It is a way of coming together with other businesses or individuals to share ideas, resources, and expertise for the benefit of all parties involved. It's a form of mentorship.

In today's fast-paced business world, it is becoming increasingly important to collaborate with niche partners who share the same vision and values as your business. It often creates a win-win situation for all parties involved. It allows businesses to tap into each other's skills, networks, and knowledge to create something new and innovative. Collaboration also helps businesses to reduce costs, increase efficiency, and improve productivity.

t can take many forms, from joint ventures, partnerships, and mergers to strategic alliances, co-creation, and co-marketing. The key is to identify the right partners who complement your business's strengths and weaknesses.

Collaboration is an essential ingredient for any business looking to grow and succeed in today's competitive business environment. By working together with niche partners, businesses can gain access to new markets, technologies, and ideas that can help them achieve their goals faster and more efficiently than they could on their own.

Understanding Niche Partnership?

Niche partnership is a mutually beneficial relationship between two businesses that operate in the same or similar industry but do not directly compete with each other. In this type of partnership, businesses share their expertise, knowledge, and resources to achieve a common goal.

For instance, a coffee shop may partner with a local bakery to offer each other's products to their customers. This way, the coffee shop can offer a wider range of food options to its customers and the bakery can reach new customers who may not have heard of them before.

Niche partnership is not only limited to the exchange of products or services but can also extend to sharing marketing strategies, customer data, and even employees. It's all about finding ways to complement each other's strengths and weaknesses to achieve a shared objective.

This type of collaboration is particularly beneficial for small businesses with limited resources, as it allows them to tap into a wider pool of expertise and resources without having to invest heavily. It also helps businesses to expand their reach and grow their customer base by tapping into each other's networks.

Niche partnership is just a smart way to foster business growth, build relationships, and achieve common goals in a mutually beneficial way.

The Difference between Collaboration and Competition

To grow your business, it's important to understand the difference between collaboration and competition. While competition involves working against one another to gain market share, collaboration involves working together towards a common goal.

In a collaboration, businesses can share their strengths and expertise to create a unique value proposition that benefits both parties. By collaborating with niche partners, businesses can gain access to new audiences, increase their brand visibility, and expand their offerings. Collaboration allows businesses to focus on their strengths while leveraging the strengths of others. For example, a web design company can collaborate with a content marketing agency to offer a comprehensive digital marketing package to clients. This benefits both businesses as they can offer a complete solution to clients while focusing on their respective areas of expertise.

On the other hand, competition can lead to a race to the bottom, with businesses undercutting each other on price and quality. By collaborating with niche partners, businesses can differentiate themselves from the competition and offer unique solutions to their customers.

So, collaboration can help you leverage the strengths of others to create unique value propositions that benefit everyone involved - yourself, your partners and your clients.

Working with niche partners can help you reach a more targeted audience and expand your reach in the market. For example, if you own a small boutique that specializes in organic skincare products, partnering with a local spa that offers organic facials could be a great collaboration. This type of partnership could involve cross-promotion, where you promote their services to your customers and they promote your products to their customers. This can lead to increased sales for both businesses and can create a win-win situation for everyone involved.

Another way collaboration with niche partners can help your business is through idea exchange. When you work with other businesses in your niche, you can share ideas, strategies, and tactics that have worked for you. It can help you learn from each other and improve your overall business operations. By collaborating with niche partners, you can also learn about new market trends or emerging technologies that can benefit your business. Collaboration with niche partners remains a powerful tool to help grow any business. By working together with others, you can reach a wider audience, share ideas and best practices, and ultimately achieve greater success in your niche market.

Benefits of Exchanging Ideas with Niche Partners

By exchanging ideas, you open up a whole new world of opportunities to grow your business. Exchanging ideas with niche partners can help you tap into new markets.

Your partner may have a customer base that you've never had access to before, and vice versa. When you share ideas and strategies, you can both benefit from each other's knowledge and experience, and reach a wider audience than you ever could alone.

Also, exchanging ideas with niche partners can help you to innovate and stay ahead of the competition. By learning from each other, you can develop new products, services or ways of working that you might not have thought of on your own. This can help you to differentiate yourself from your competitors, and stay ahead of the curve.

Finally, exchanging ideas with niche partners can help you to build relationships and trust with other businesses in your industry. By working together, you can build a sense of camaraderie and mutual respect, which can lead to future opportunities for collaboration and growth.

Identifying Potential Niche Partners for Collaboration

In identifying potential niche partners for collaboration, the key is to think outside the box. It's not always about finding businesses that are similar to yours, but rather those that complement what you offer.

Start by researching businesses within your industry or niche that offer products or services that would be of interest to your target audience. Look for businesses that share similar values and have a similar target market. Check out social media groups, online forums, and other online communities where people in your industry or niche gather. Engage with other business owners and entrepreneurs and start building relationships.

Another approach is to look for businesses that operate in related industries or niches. For example, if you run a pet grooming business, you could collaborate with a local pet store, a dog-walking service, or even a dog trainer. By partnering with businesses that offer complementary services, you can create a complete package for your customers and offer them a more comprehensive experience.

When considering potential niche partners, it's important to assess their reputation and credibility. Look for businesses that are well-established, have a good track record, and have a strong online presence. You want to collaborate with businesses that share your values and that you would be proud to be associated with.

Never be afraid to approach potential partners directly. Reach out to them via email or social media, introduce yourself and your business, and explain why you think a collaboration would be beneficial. Be clear about what you can offer and what you hope to gain from the partnership. With a little bit of effort and creativity, you can identify and build relationships with niche partners that will help you grow your business.

Approaching niche partners for collaboration can seem daunting, but it doesn't have to be. The secret to successful collaborations is to approach potential partners with an open mind and a willingness to work together towards a common goal. Here are some tips to consider when reaching out to potential partners:

1. Research potential partners: Take time to research potential partners that align with your brand and target audience. Look for businesses that complement your products or services, and that have a similar target audience.
2. Establish a relationship: Before jumping into a collaboration, start by establishing a relationship with potential partners. Follow them on social media, engage with their content, and attend events they are hosting or attending. It builds trust and rapport before you approach them for collaboration.
3. Personalize your approach: When reaching out to potential partners, avoid sending generic emails or messages. Take the time to personalize your approach and explain why you think a collaboration would be beneficial for both parties.
4. Be clear about your proposal: When proposing a collaboration, be clear about your expectations and what you can offer. Outline the benefits of the collaboration, and how it will help both businesses grow.
5. Be open to negotiation: Collaborations should be a win-win for both parties, so be open to negotiation. Listen to the needs and goals of potential partners, and work together to create a collaboration that works for everyone.

Best Practices for Successful Collaboration with Niche Partners

Collaborating with niche partners can be an incredibly effective way to grow your business. However, it's important to approach these partnerships with the right mindset and strategies to ensure success. Identify partners that align with your business values and goals. Look for partners that complement your products or services and have a similar target audience. This will ensure that the collaboration is mutually beneficial.

You should also plan and communicate clearly with your partners. Define the goals and expectations for the partnership, including timelines, responsibilities, and outcomes. That helps to avoid misunderstandings and ensure that everyone is working towards the same goal.

Be open to new ideas and feedback. Collaboration is about idea exchange and learning from each other. Be willing to listen to your partners' suggestions and feedback, and be open to trying new things.

Be sure to measure the success of the collaboration. Set clear metrics for success and track progress towards those goals. It helps to determine if the partnership is working and if any adjustments need to be made.

When you follow these practices, you can create successful collaborations with niche partners that can help grow your business and reach new audiences.

Measure the Success of Niche Partnerships

Measuring the success of niche partnerships is essential to ensure that both parties are benefiting from the collaboration. There are several ways to measure the success of a partnership, and it's important to set goals and track progress towards those goals.

One way to measure success is through increased revenue or sales. By tracking sales and revenue generated from the partnership, you can determine if it's worth continuing the partnership or not. It's also important to track any costs associated with the partnership to ensure that it's profitable for both parties.

One other way to measure success is through increased brand awareness. This can be done by tracking website traffic, social media engagement, and any other metrics that can show an increase in brand visibility. If you see an increase in brand awareness, it's a good sign that the partnership is working.

Customer feedback is also an important metric to track. By gathering feedback from customers who have interacted with the partnership, you can determine if the partnership is resonating with your target audience. This feedback can be collected through surveys, reviews, and social media comments.

Lastly, if the partnership is generating new leads or customers, it's a clear sign that it's successful. By tracking new leads and customers, you can determine the ROI of the partnership and decide if it's worth continuing.

Measuring the success of niche partnerships is essential to ensure that both parties are benefiting from the collaboration. As you track revenue, brand awareness, customer feedback, and new leads, you will be able to determine if the partnership is working and make adjustments as needed.

In conclusion, niche partnership is a great way to grow your business and expand your reach. By collaborating with other businesses in your industry, you can exchange ideas, share resources, and tap into each other's audiences to reach new customers. This approach is especially effective for small businesses and startups that may not have the resources to compete with larger companies on their own. By working together, you can combine your strengths and overcome your weaknesses to create a stronger, more competitive brand.

Looking to the future, there is enormous potential for niche partnerships to continue to drive business growth. As the economy and marketplace become more complex, businesses will need to find new and innovative ways to stay ahead of the competition. Niche partnerships provide a promising avenue for doing just that.

As you consider potential niche partnerships, be sure to think carefully about the benefits that each partner can bring to the table. Look for businesses that share your values, are aligned with your goals, and offer complementary products or services. With the right niche partnerships in place, the sky's the limit for your business growth potential.

What we have today is a fast-paced business world. It's easy to get caught up in competition and forget about the benefits of collaboration. When you exchange ideas with other businesses, particularly those in your niche, you tap into new markets, develop new products, and ultimately grow your business in a sustainable way. For a better result, you should combine this with mentorship. Having a knowledgeable and supportive mentor can make all the difference in achieving your goals and advancing your career. It is essential to find a mentor who aligns with your values and has experience in your industry.

Chapter 11

Take on PEOPLE with Skills

Your Business Needs Highly Skilled and Passionate Workers

Every successful business has one thing in common: highly skilled and passionate workers. These two qualities go hand in hand and are essential for any company that wants to thrive in today's competitive market. Passionate employees are those who are genuinely excited about their work and the company they work for. They are eager to learn and grow, and they are always looking for ways to improve their skills. On the other hand, highly skilled employees are those who have the necessary knowledge and experience to perform their job at a high level. When you combine these two qualities, you get a workforce that is highly motivated, productive, and dedicated to achieving the company's goals.

Highly skilled and passionate workers are the driving force behind any successful business. They are the ones who bring innovation, creativity, and a sense of purpose to their work. These workers not only have the necessary skills to complete their tasks, but also a deep connection to the work they do. When employees are passionate about their work, they are more likely to go above and beyond just completing their tasks. They will strive to make a difference, to make an impact, and to continuously improve.

Having passionate and skilled workers means that your business will have a competitive edge. They will bring fresh ideas to the table, and constantly look for ways to improve processes and products.

Their drive and dedication will translate into higher quality work, better customer service, and increased productivity. This will ultimately lead to increased profitability and growth for your business.

Furthermore, passionate and skilled workers are more likely to stay with a company for a longer period of time. They are invested in their work, and they want to see the company succeed. This means lower employee turnover rates, which can save businesses time and money in recruitment and training costs.

Having highly skilled and passionate workers is a key ingredient to the success of any business. They bring energy, creativity, and dedication to their work, which in turn creates a positive work environment and helps your business thrive.

Passion is a crucial ingredient in the success of any business. Passionate employees bring energy, enthusiasm, and creativity to the workplace which translates into increased productivity, engagement, and positive work culture. Passionate employees are willing to go above and beyond their job description to make sure that the job is done right. They are more likely to take ownership of their work and feel pride in the results they achieve.

Passionate employees are also more committed to the goals and objectives of the company. They are more likely to stay with the company longer and become advocates for the brand. They believe in what the company stands for and are more likely to promote it to others. Having passionate employees sets a positive tone for the entire organization. It fosters a culture of innovation, creativity, and excellence. Passionate employees inspire others to push themselves to be their best and to strive for excellence in everything they do.

The importance of skill in the workplace

Skills are absolutely essential in the workplace, no matter the industry or business size. They are the backbone of a high-performing team and play a crucial role in achieving business success. Having skilled workers on board means that they have the knowledge, experience, and technical ability to carry out their roles effectively and efficiently. When you have a workforce that possesses the right skills, you can expect a significant improvement in productivity, quality, and output.

Moreover, skillful employees are more likely to take the initiative and ownership of their work. They are confident in their abilities and are willing to go the extra mile to achieve the best possible results. This not only benefits the company but also contributes to their personal and professional growth.

Investing in training and development programs for your workforce can also help to enhance their skills and keep them up to date with the latest technologies and trends. This can turn your business into an industry leader and keep you ahead of your competitors.

The importance of skill in the workplace cannot be overstated. It is essential to have a workforce that possesses the right skills to ensure efficiency, productivity, and quality. By investing in training and development programs for your team, you can create a skilled workforce that is capable of taking your business to new heights.

Having highly skilled and passionate workers in your business can be a game-changer. They bring a level of expertise and energy to the table that can propel your business to new heights.

One of the biggest advantages of having highly skilled workers is that they are capable of completing tasks quickly and with precision. They have a deep understanding of the industry and the latest trends, which enables them to complete tasks efficiently and creatively. This not only increases the quality of the work but also reduces the turnaround time, which is an important factor in today's fast-paced business environment.

Besides their technical skills, passionate workers are also more likely to be engaged and committed to their work. They take pride in their work and are invested in the success of the company. This level of dedication often results in higher levels of productivity and better quality work.

Another advantage of having highly skilled and passionate workers is that they can act as ambassadors for your brand. They are the face of your business and can represent your brand in a positive light. They have the knowledge and expertise to answer customer questions and provide excellent customer service, which can help to build brand loyalty and increase customer satisfaction.

Having highly skilled and passionate workers can lead to increased productivity, better quality work, and a stronger brand image. So, it's important to invest in your employees and provide them with the tools and resources they need to be successful.

How to Identify Highly Skilled and Passionate Workers

Identifying highly skilled and passionate workers during recruitment can be a challenging task, but it is definitely worth the effort. Here are some tips to help you identify the best candidates. By following these tips, you can identify highly skilled and passionate workers who will add value to your business and help you achieve your goals:

Look for relevant experience

You should look for candidates who have experience in the field or industry you are recruiting for. This will give you a good indication that they have the relevant skills and knowledge needed for the job.

Check their qualifications

Many jobs require specific qualifications or certifications, so it is important to check that the candidate has the necessary qualifications. This will give you confidence that they have the required knowledge and skills for the job.

Check their references

Always check the candidate's references to get a sense of their work ethic, reliability, and enthusiasm. You can get valuable insights into their passion for the job and how they work in a team.

Ask behavioral questions

During the interview process, ask behavioral questions to get a sense of how the candidate approaches tasks, handles challenges, and works with others. This will give you insight into their work style and passion for the job.

Look for passion and enthusiasm

Passionate workers are highly motivated, enthusiastic, and energetic. Look for candidates who show a genuine interest in the job and the industry. They are likely to be highly skilled, productive, and committed to delivering high-quality work.

How Do You foster passion and skill development in your workforce?

Fostering passion and skill development in your workforce should be a top priority for every business. It all starts with a company culture that values continuous learning and growth. One of the best ways to do this is to offer training and development opportunities for your employees. This can include in-house training sessions, online courses, or workshops and conferences. Encourage your employees to attend these events and provide support for them to do so. By investing in your employees, you show them that you value their growth and development.

It is vital that you create a work environment that encourages creativity and innovation. Allow your employees the freedom to experiment and try new things, and provide them with the resources and support they need to do so. This can be as simple as providing access to new software or tools, or as complex as restructuring your team to allow for more collaboration and cross-functional projects.

Also ensure you recognize and reward your employees for their hard work and contributions. This can be through promotions, bonuses, or simply a heartfelt thank you. When your employees feel valued and appreciated, they are more likely to be passionate about their work and continue to develop their skills.

Strategies for Creating a Passion-Driven Work Environment

Creating a passion-driven work environment is essential for businesses looking to harness the power of highly skilled and passionate workers. The following are some effective strategies for doing so:

1. **Hire passionate people:** It all starts with the hiring process. Look for candidates who have a genuine passion for the industry or field you're in. This can be gauged through their resume, cover letter, and interview. Passionate individuals are more likely to be committed to their work and will be motivated to give their best effort each day.
2. **Encourage autonomy:** Highly skilled and passionate workers thrive on autonomy. Allow them to take ownership of their work and encourage them to take initiatives. This will not only allow them to utilize their skills to the fullest but also lead to greater job satisfaction and fulfillment.
3. **Provide growth opportunities:** Top performers are always looking for ways to grow and develop their skills. Providing opportunities for training, attending conferences, and taking on new challenges can keep them engaged and motivated.
4. **Foster a positive work culture:** A positive work culture is essential for creating a passion-driven work environment. Encourage open communication, respect, collaboration, and celebrate successes. This creates a sense of belonging and makes the workplace a more enjoyable and fulfilling place to be.

Once you have highly skilled and passionate workers on your team, it's essential to nurture and retain them if you want your business to thrive. How do you go about this?

1. **Encourage their growth:** Provide opportunities for your employees to learn new skills and take on new challenges. This could be through training, conferences, or even job shadowing. When employees feel like they're growing and advancing, they're more likely to stay with your company.
2. **Recognize their contributions:** Make sure your employees know that their hard work is appreciated. This can be through simple gestures like thank-you notes or public recognition at team meetings. When employees feel valued and recognized, they're more likely to stay motivated and engaged.
3. **Create a positive work environment:** A positive work environment can make a huge difference in employee satisfaction. This includes things like providing a comfortable workspace, promoting work-life balance, and fostering positive relationships among team members.
4. **Offer competitive compensation and benefits:** While money isn't everything, it's important to offer competitive compensation and benefits packages to your employees. This includes things like fair salaries, health insurance, and retirement plans. When employees feel like they're being fairly compensated for their work, they're more likely to stick around.

Examples of Brand Reaping These Benefits

There are numerous real-world examples of businesses that have benefited greatly from having highly skilled and passionate workers on their team. One such example is Apple, which is known for its innovative and cutting-edge technology. Steve Jobs, the founder of Apple, was known for his passion and drive in creating products that were not only functional but also aesthetically pleasing. This passion and drive were reflected in the company's culture, and Apple was able to hire and retain some of the most talented engineers and designers in the industry.

Another example is Zappos, an online shoe and clothing retailer. Zappos is known for its excellent customer service, and part of this success can be attributed to the passion and skill of its employees. Zappos takes great care in hiring people who are not only skilled but also passionate about helping customers. This passion is reflected in the company's culture, which values customer service above all else.

Finally, we have Tesla, a company that is leading the way in the electric vehicle market. Elon Musk, the founder of Tesla, is known for his passion for renewable energy and his desire to change the world. This passion has been reflected in the company's culture, and Tesla has been able to attract and retain some of the most talented engineers and designers in the industry.

The examples above show that having passionate and skilled workers can be a significant advantage for any company. Not only do these workers bring their expertise to the table, but they also bring a level of enthusiasm and drive that can be infectious and inspiring to others. When a culture of passion and skill is fostered, businesses will attract and retain the best talent, and ultimately, achieve greater success.

So, there's no doubt that highly skilled and passionate workers are a valuable asset to any business. These individuals bring energy, creativity, and a strong work ethic that can take your business to new heights. By harnessing the power of passion and skill, you can build a team that is highly motivated and driven to succeed.

When looking for new hires, it's important to prioritize these qualities alongside relevant experience and qualifications. You want to make sure that your team members share your vision and are committed to achieving your goals. It's also important to create a work environment that fosters creativity and collaboration, where team members can share ideas and build on each other's strengths.

Investing in the development of your team members is also critical. By offering training and development opportunities, you can help your employees grow both personally and professionally, while also strengthening their skills and expertise. This not only benefits them personally, but it also benefits your business as you will have a team that is constantly improving and evolving.

Harnessing the power of passion and skill is essential for any business that wants to thrive and succeed in today's competitive market. By prioritizing these qualities and creating a supportive work environment, you can build a team that is highly motivated, skilled, and committed to achieving your business goals.

Chapter 12

How Can We Do This INSTEAD of I CAN'T Do This

How Optimism Can Help You Achieve Your Goals: The Science Behind Positive Thinking

We all have goals and aspirations, but sometimes it can be difficult to stay motivated and focused. The power of positive thinking is a popular topic, but it's often dismissed as mere fluff. However, science has shown that optimism can have a profound impact on our ability to achieve our goals.

In this chapter, we will discuss the science behind positive thinking and how it can help you achieve your goals. From the benefits of a positive mindset to practical techniques for cultivating optimism, I will provide you with the tools you need to stay motivated, focused, and optimistic on your journey to success.

The power of optimism in achieving goals

Positive thinking has been praised for its ability to help people achieve their goals and live happier lives. Optimism is a state of mind that allows individuals to see the world in a positive light, focusing on the good rather than the bad. This mindset can have profound effects on an individual's physical and emotional health, as well as on their ability to achieve their goals.

Studies have shown that positive thinking leads to a range of benefits, including reduced stress levels, improved immunity, and increased overall happiness. Moreover, optimists are more likely to persevere in the face of challenges, as they believe that they can overcome obstacles and achieve their goals. This can lead to greater success in both personal and professional endeavors.

In contrast, individuals who adopt a negative mindset are more likely to experience stress, depression, and other negative emotions. These individuals are more likely to give up in the face of challenges and may struggle to achieve their goals.

The power of positive thinking is not just a matter of "looking on the bright side." It is a mindset that can be cultivated through intentional practices such as gratitude journaling, visualization, and positive self-talk. By fostering a positive outlook on life, individuals can improve their physical and emotional health, increase their resilience, and achieve greater success in their personal and professional lives.

When it comes to optimism, it's not just a matter of having a positive outlook on life. There is actually scientific evidence to suggest that positive thinking can have a significant impact on both your brain and body. Studies have shown that people who practice positive thinking tend to have lower levels of stress hormones like cortisol. This can have a range of positive effects on the body, including reducing inflammation, improving immune function, and even lowering the risk of chronic diseases like heart disease and diabetes.

In addition to its physical benefits, positive thinking can also have a significant impact on mental health. Optimistic people tend to have better coping skills and are better able to manage stress and anxiety. They also tend to have higher levels of resilience, which allows them to bounce back from setbacks more quickly.

But how does positive thinking actually impact the brain?

Research has shown that when we practice optimism, our brains release a range of neurotransmitters and hormones that are associated with positive emotions. These include dopamine, serotonin, and endorphins, which can create feelings of happiness, pleasure, and contentment.

The science behind optimism is clear: cultivating a positive mindset can have a range of benefits for both your physical and mental health. So if you're looking to achieve your goals, it's worth considering how you can incorporate more positive thinking into your daily life.

Optimism vs. pessimism: The Differences and How They Affect Your Goal achievement

Optimism and pessimism are two attitudes that can greatly affect your ability to achieve your goals. Optimists tend to see setbacks as temporary and believe they can overcome obstacles. They view these challenges as opportunities for growth and learning, which can help them stay motivated and committed to their goals. On the other hand, pessimists tend to see setbacks as permanent and believe that they have little control over their circumstances. They may give up easily when faced with obstacles, feeling defeated and disheartened about their ability to achieve their goals.

Research has shown that optimists are more likely to achieve their goals compared to pessimists. This is because optimism allows individuals to maintain a positive mindset and focus on solutions rather than problems. Optimists also tend to be more persistent and resilient in the face of challenges, which helps them stay motivated and committed to their goals.

However, it's important to note that being overly optimistic can also have its drawbacks. When individuals are too optimistic, they may underestimate the amount of effort required to achieve their goals and may not adequately prepare for potential obstacles. This can lead to disappointment and frustration when they encounter setbacks.

Optimism can be a powerful tool for achieving your goals. By adopting an optimistic attitude, you can stay motivated, focused, and resilient in the face of challenges. However, it's important to maintain a realistic perspective and be prepared for potential obstacles along the way.

But cultivating optimism is not an overnight process, but it is definitely attainable with the right mindset and tools in place. Here are some practical tips to help you become more positive:

Practice gratitude

Start each day by acknowledging the things in your life that you are grateful for. This simple exercise can help shift your focus from what you lack to what you have, fostering a more positive outlook.

Challenge negative thoughts

When you find yourself thinking negatively, challenge those thoughts by asking yourself if they are really true. Often negative thoughts are based on assumptions or limited information, and reframing them in a more positive light can help shift your mindset.

Surround yourself with positivity

Spend time with people who uplift and inspire you. Seek out positive role models, mentors, or friends who can offer encouragement and support.

Focus on solutions

When faced with a problem or challenge, focus on finding solutions rather than dwelling on the problem itself. This proactive approach can help build confidence and a sense of control over your life.

Practice self-care

Take care of yourself physically and mentally by eating well, exercising regularly, getting enough sleep, and engaging in activities that bring you joy and fulfillment.

By incorporating these practical tips into your daily routine, you can slowly but surely cultivate a more positive and optimistic outlook on life. With time and effort, you may find that your newfound positivity helps you achieve your goals and live a more fulfilling life.

The Role of Self-Talk: How Your Inner Dialogue Can affect Your Mindset and Goals

One of the most important aspects of positive thinking is your self-talk. The way you talk to yourself has a profound impact on your mindset, which in turn affects your actions and ultimately your results.

Negative self-talk can be a major obstacle to achieving your goals. It can lower your self-esteem, limit your possibilities, and even prevent you from taking action. On the other hand, positive self-talk can help you stay motivated, enhance your confidence, and give you the push you need to keep going when things get tough.

So, how can you develop positive self-talk? Start by paying attention to your inner dialogue. Whenever you catch yourself thinking negatively, reframe the thought in a positive way. For example, instead of saying "I can't do this," say "I may face challenges, but I will find a way to overcome them." This simple shift in your self-talk can make a big difference in your mindset and your ability to achieve your goals. Another technique is to use affirmations. Affirmations are positive statements that you repeat to yourself regularly to reinforce positive beliefs and attitudes.

For example, you might say "I am capable of achieving my goals" or "I am worthy of success." By repeating these affirmations to yourself on a regular basis, you can start to shift your mindset towards a more positive, optimistic outlook.

Retain this in your mind always: your thoughts have power. By changing your self-talk and cultivating a more positive mindset, you can set yourself up for success and achieve your goals with greater ease and confidence.

Overcoming Obstacles with Optimism

Overcoming obstacles is an inevitable part of any journey to achieving your goals. However, it's important to approach these obstacles with optimism, rather than allowing them to bring you down. One strategy to help you stay positive when faced with challenges is to reframe the situation in a positive light. Instead of seeing the obstacle as a roadblock, try to view it as an opportunity to learn and grow. This can help shift your mindset from one of frustration to one of positivity and determination.

Another strategy is to practice mindfulness and present-moment awareness. When faced with a challenge, it's easy to get caught up in negative thoughts and emotions. By focusing on the present moment and staying grounded in the here and now, you can prevent yourself from getting lost in a spiral of negativity. This can help you maintain a sense of perspective and cope with the challenge in a more constructive way.

You should cultivate a support network of people who believe in you and your goals. Surrounding yourself with positive, supportive individuals can help you stay motivated and maintain a positive outlook, even when faced with obstacles. Whether it's friends, family, or a professional coach or mentor, having a support system in place can make all the difference in helping you overcome challenges and achieve your goals.

So, the key to overcoming obstacles with optimism is to cultivate a mindset of resilience and determination. By focusing on the positive, staying present and mindful, and building a support network, you can develop the inner strength and optimism needed to overcome any obstacle and achieve your goals.

Visualization: How Imagining Success can Help You Achieve Goals

Visualization is a powerful tool that can help you turn your optimistic thoughts into reality. By visualizing your success, you are essentially training your mind to think positively and believe that achieving your goals is possible. Your brain will start to look for ways to make your vision a reality, and you'll find yourself naturally taking actions that will help you achieve your goals.

When you visualize your success, it's important to be as specific as possible. Imagine yourself in the situation you want to be in, and think about all the details: what you're wearing, who is with you, what you're saying, how you're feeling. The more vividly you can imagine yourself in that situation, the more real it will feel to you, and the more motivated you'll be to make it happen.

Visualization can also help you overcome obstacles and challenges that might stand in your way. By visualizing yourself overcoming these obstacles, you'll be better equipped to face them when they arise in real life. You'll be able to approach them with a positive attitude, knowing that you have the skills and resources to overcome them.

So, take some time every day to visualize your success. Picture yourself achieving your goals, and don't be afraid to dream big. The more you focus on your optimistic thoughts and visualize your success, the more likely you are to achieve your goals and live the life you want.

Gratitude: a Channel to Optimism and Goal Achievement

Gratitude is the feeling of being thankful and appreciative of the good things in your life. It is a powerful emotion that has been shown to improve optimism and help achieve goals. When you are grateful, you are focusing on the positive aspects of your life and this can help you to develop a more positive outlook.

Research has shown that practicing gratitude can improve mental health, increase happiness, and reduce stress levels. When you are feeling stressed or overwhelmed, taking a moment to think about the things you are thankful for can help to shift your focus to the positive and reduce feelings of anxiety.

In addition to improving mental health, gratitude can also help you to achieve your goals. When you are grateful for what you have, you are more likely to be content with your current situation, which can help to reduce feelings of frustration and anxiety. This can make it easier to set and achieve goals, as you are not constantly focused on what you don't have.

Gratitude can also help to improve relationships, as it encourages you to focus on the positive aspects of your interactions with others. When you are grateful for the people in your life, you are more likely to show appreciation and kindness, which can help to strengthen relationships and build a support network. Incorporating gratitude into your daily routine can be as simple as taking a few minutes each day to reflect on the things you are thankful for. This can help to improve your optimism, reduce stress levels, and improve your chances of achieving your goals.

What the Combination of Optimism and Resilience can Do

Optimism and resilience are two important factors that can help you bounce back from setbacks. When you face challenges or setbacks in your life, it's easy to get bogged down in negative thinking and lose sight of your goals. However, by cultivating a positive outlook and focusing on the opportunities presented by setbacks, you can build your resilience and keep moving forward. Research has shown that optimistic individuals are better able to cope with stress and adversity. They are more likely to view setbacks as temporary and specific rather than permanent and pervasive, which helps them to stay motivated and focused on their goals. In addition, optimists tend to be more proactive in seeking out solutions to problems, which can help them to overcome obstacles more quickly.

A major factor in resilience is the ability to learn from failure. By reframing failure as an opportunity to learn and grow, you can turn setbacks into stepping stones to success. This requires a positive mindset and a willingness to embrace challenges and take risks. With practice, you can develop the resilience and optimism needed to bounce back from setbacks and achieve your goals.

Generally, optimism is a powerful tool that can help you achieve your goals and live a happier, more fulfilling life. It's not just a vague concept or a feel-good emotion, but a scientifically proven phenomenon that has been shown to have a real impact on our thoughts, behaviors, and outcomes.

When you cultivate a positive mindset and focus on the possibilities rather than the limitations, you overcome obstacles, learn from our mistakes, and find creative solutions to challenges. You will also build better relationships, enjoy better health, and experience greater success in all areas of our lives.

Of course, optimism alone won't guarantee success, and we still need to put in the hard work and make smart choices. But with a mindset of positivity and possibility, we can approach our goals and challenges with greater resilience, energy, and enthusiasm.

So whether you're striving for a big career goal, working to improve your relationships, or simply seeking more joy and fulfillment in your daily life, cultivating optimism can be a powerful and transformative practice. Give it a try and see what positive changes it can bring to your life!

CHAPTER 13

Have the Passion and Have Success

Drawing Inspiration from the Ray Croc Story

Ray Kroc's name may not be familiar to many people, but his most famous creation certainly is. As the founder of McDonald's, Kroc is responsible for one of the most successful and recognizable brands in the world today. But how did a milkshake machine salesman become a global business icon? The answer lies in Kroc's tenacity and unwavering belief in his ability to create something extraordinary. In this post, we'll explore Kroc's journey, from his humble beginnings to his incredible success with McDonald's, and the lessons we can learn from his story. We'll also take a closer look at the book that inspired Kroc, "Think and Grow Rich," and how its principles helped shape his mindset and approach to business. So, buckle up, and let's dive into the fascinating story of Ray Kroc.

Who is Ray Kroc?

Ray Kroc is a pioneer in the fast-food industry and is widely known for turning McDonald's into the global brand it is today. Kroc had a humble beginning, and his early years were spent working as a salesman and playing the piano at a local bar. Eventually, he became a milkshake machine salesman and that's where his life changed forever. In 1954, he visited a small but popular fast-food restaurant in San Bernardino, California, owned by Richard and Maurice McDonald.

Kroc was fascinated by their unique assembly-line system, which served food quickly and efficiently. He saw the potential to replicate their success and convinced the brothers to let him franchise their restaurant. Kroc's vision and business acumen led him to take over the McDonald's brand and turned it into a global giant. His story is one of perseverance, hard work, and a willingness to take risks. He is an inspiration to entrepreneurs everywhere, and his legacy continues to impact the fast-food industry to this day.

The early life of Ray Kroc and his struggles

Ray Kroc was born in Illinois in 1902, and his parents were of Czech origin. Due to financial difficulties, he was forced to leave school at the age of 15 and get a job. He worked in various positions, such as a paper cup salesman and a jazz musician, but never found his true calling.

After serving in the army during World War I, he returned to work as a salesman, selling products such as milkshake machines. It was during this time that he met the McDonald brothers, who owned a small fast-food restaurant in California. Kroc was impressed by the efficiency of their operation and saw the potential for the concept to become a national franchise.

However, the McDonald brothers were initially resistant to the idea of franchising their business, so Kroc had to find a way to convince them. He eventually succeeded and opened his first franchise in 1955. However, he faced many challenges along the way, such as financial difficulties and disagreements with the McDonald brothers.

Despite these struggles, Kroc persevered and worked tirelessly to make his business a success. He eventually bought out the McDonald brothers and turned McDonald's into a global brand that is now one of the most recognizable and successful companies in the world. Kroc's story is a testament to the power of determination and hard work in achieving success.

How Ray Kroc discovered "Think and Grow Rich"

As a struggling milkshake mixer salesman in the 1950s, Ray Kroc stumbled upon a copy of the book "Think and Grow Rich" by

Napoleon Hill during a business trip. This book, which had been published more than 20 years earlier, had a profound impact on Kroc's life and business ventures. "Think and Grow Rich" emphasizes the importance of having a positive mindset, persistence, and determination in achieving success. Kroc took these lessons to heart and applied them to his business pursuits, particularly in his desire to franchise the McDonald's brand.

Kroc became obsessed with the idea of expanding the McDonald's chain, despite pushback from the original owners. He persisted and eventually bought out the franchise rights from the McDonald brothers, and the rest is history.

Kroc credited "Think and Grow Rich" with providing him with the motivation and inspiration to take his business to the next level. His story serves as a testament to the power of positive thinking and the impact that a single book can have on one's life and career.

"Think and Grow Rich" by Napoleon Hill is an influential book that has helped shape the mindset of many successful businesspeople. Ray Kroc, the founder of McDonald's, is one of them.

In his autobiography, "Grinding It Out," Kroc credits "Think and Grow Rich" with helping him develop the persistence, determination, and vision necessary to build a global empire. He read the book several times throughout his life, and it became a constant source of inspiration and motivation for him.

The book's central message of "whatever the mind can conceive and believe, it can achieve" resonated deeply with Kroc. He believed that if he could imagine something, he could make it a reality through hard work, perseverance, and a willingness to take risks.

Kroc also adopted the book's principles of goal-setting and visualization. He had a clear vision of what he wanted to achieve with McDonald's, and he worked tirelessly to make that vision a reality. He also believed in the power of positive thinking and surrounded himself with like-minded individuals who shared his vision and dedication.

To sum it up, "Think and Grow Rich" played a significant role in shaping Ray Kroc's mindset and approach to business. It helped him to think big, set ambitious goals, and persist in the face of challenges and setbacks. Without these qualities, it's unlikely that he would have been able to achieve the success he did with McDonald's.

How Ray Kroc Turned a Small Burger Restaurant into a Global Empire

Ray Kroc was a true visionary and entrepreneur who took a small burger restaurant and turned it into a global empire. His story is a testament to the power of perseverance, hard work, and determination. In the 1950s, Kroc was still a struggling milkshake machine salesman who stumbled upon a small but successful restaurant in San Bernardino, California, run by two brothers named Richard and Maurice McDonald.

As earlier stated, Kroc was impressed by the brothers' innovative "Speedee Service System" that used efficient assembly line techniques to serve burgers, fries, and milkshakes quickly and inexpensively. He saw the potential for the restaurant to be replicated and expanded across the country.

Kroc convinced the McDonald brothers to let him franchise their concept, and in 1955 he opened his first McDonald's restaurant in Des Plaines, Illinois. It was an instant success, and Kroc soon began opening more and more franchises across the country. He was a tireless promoter of the brand, and he was always looking for new ways to improve the restaurant experience for customers.

One of Kroc's most significant contributions to the company was his focus on standardization. He wanted every McDonald's restaurant to look and feel the same, no matter where it was located. He created a detailed operations manual that spelled out everything from the size of the french fries to the way the employees should greet customers. This made it easy for franchisees to open and operate their restaurants, and it ensured that customers would have a consistent experience at every McDonald's they visited.

Kroc's relentless expansion of the McDonald's empire was not without its challenges. He had to deal with franchisees who didn't follow the rules, competitors who tried to copy his concept, and criticisms from health advocates who accused McDonald's of contributing to the obesity epidemic. Despite these challenges, Kroc remained committed to his vision of making McDonald's the most popular fast-food chain in the world.

Today, McDonald's has over 38,000 restaurants in more than 100 countries, and it serves over 69 million customers every day. The company's success is a testament to the entrepreneurial spirit and business acumen of Ray Kroc, who took a small burger restaurant and turned it into a global phenomenon.

Did You See Persistence and Determination in Ray Kroc's Success Story?

Persistence and determination are two of the most important qualities that contributed to Ray Kroc's successful journey. Ray Kroc was known for his never-give-up attitude and his relentless pursuit of his goals. Despite facing numerous rejections and setbacks, he remained persistent in his efforts to grow his business.

In the early days of McDonald's, Kroc faced several obstacles, including a lack of funds and resistance from franchisees who weren't willing to adopt his business model. Despite these challenges, Kroc remained determined to grow his business and find a way to make it work.

Kroc's persistence and determination were evident in his work ethic. He was known to work long hours and tirelessly pursue new opportunities to expand his business. Kroc was also willing to take calculated risks and make bold decisions, such as purchasing land and leasing it to his franchisees, which allowed him to generate additional revenue streams.

In the end, Kroc's persistence and determination paid off. He turned McDonald's into a global brand that is now recognized around the world. Kroc's story is a testament to the power of determination and the importance of never giving up on your dreams.

The Leadership Style and Business Philosophy that Helped Ray Kroc

Ray Kroc's leadership style and business philosophy were instrumental in the success of McDonald's. Kroc was known for his strong work ethic, determination, and tenacity. He was a firm believer in the American Dream and the idea that hard work and persistence could lead to success. He brought this philosophy to his leadership style, often working long hours and pushing himself and his team to achieve their goals.

Kroc was also a proponent of franchising, which allowed McDonald's to rapidly expand across the United States and eventually the world. He believed in creating a consistent customer experience across all franchises and worked closely with franchisees to ensure that they adhered to the McDonald's system.

Another major aspect of Kroc's leadership style was his emphasis on customer service. He believed that happy customers were the key to the success of any business and worked tirelessly to ensure that McDonald's provided a quality experience for every customer. This emphasis on customer service led to innovations such as the creation of the drive-thru and the development of new menu items to meet customer demand.

Ray Kroc's leadership style and business philosophy played a crucial role in the success of McDonald's. His dedication to hard work, franchising, and customer service created a legacy that continues to shape the fast-food industry and inspire entrepreneurs around the world.

His Challenges and How He Overcame Them

Ray Kroc's journey to success was not an easy one. He faced numerous hurdles and challenges throughout his career but he never gave up.

One of the biggest obstacles he encountered was convincing franchisees to adhere to his stringent standards. Ray was a stickler for consistency in everything, from the burger patties to the way the fries were cooked. He wanted every customer to receive the same high-quality experience regardless of which location they visited. However, this was easier said than done, as many franchisees wanted to do things their own way.

Another challenge Ray faced was expanding the business globally. When Ray first started franchising, he focused solely on the United States. However, he soon realized that if he wanted to grow the business, he needed to look beyond the borders of America. This led to him opening his first international location in Canada in 1967. But, opening locations in different countries brought its own set of challenges, such as navigating different cultures, customs, and regulations.

Despite the challenges, Ray never lost sight of his goals. He was always looking for new ways to innovate and improve the business. One of his most significant contributions was the creation of the Hamburger University in 1961. This was a training facility where franchisees and employees could learn the ins and outs of the business. It was also a way to promote consistency and ensure that every location adhered to the same high standards.

In the end, Ray's determination and hard work paid off. Today, McDonald's is a global brand with over 37,000 locations in more than 100 countries. Ray Kroc's story is proof that with the right mindset, anything is possible.

His Legacy and Impact on the Fast-Food Industry

Ray Kroc's legacy and impact on the fast-food industry is undeniable. He was a true visionary who revolutionized the fast-food industry and turned McDonald's into a global brand.

Kroc's business philosophy was simple yet effective: provide customers with quality food, fast service, and affordable prices. He also believed in standardizing the fast-food experience, which meant that customers could expect the same quality food and service at any McDonald's restaurant, no matter where they were in the world. The introduction of the famous "Golden Arches" logo is also credited to Kroc. The logo became synonymous with the brand and is still recognizable worldwide.

Under Kroc's leadership, McDonald's grew to become the largest fast-food chain in the world, with restaurants in over 100 countries. The company has also become a cultural icon, with its influence extending beyond the fast-food industry.

Kroc's success story is a testament to the power of determination, hard work, and innovation. His legacy continues to inspire entrepreneurs around the world to this day.

Lessons from Ray Kroc's Journey from Reading "Think and Grow Rich" to Becoming a Global Business Owner

Ray Kroc's journey from "Think and Grow Rich" to global business is an inspiring one, full of valuable lessons for any aspiring entrepreneur. One of the key takeaways from his story is the power of persistence. Despite facing numerous setbacks and rejections, Kroc remained determined to achieve his goals and never gave up on his vision of turning McDonald's into a global empire.

One other impressive lesson is the value of continuous learning and self-improvement. Kroc was a voracious reader and was always seeking new knowledge and insights that could help him improve both himself and his business. He understood that success is a journey, not a destination, and that staying curious and open-minded is key to staying ahead of the curve in any industry.

Kroc's story also highlights the importance of strong leadership and a clear sense of purpose. He was a charismatic and visionary leader who was able to inspire his team to share his passion for serving customers and delivering high-quality products. He also had a crystal-clear vision for what he wanted to achieve with McDonald's, and was relentless in pursuing that vision even in the face of opposition from his own board of directors.

The lessons learned from Ray Kroc's journey can be applied to any business or personal endeavor. By staying persistent, continuously learning and improving, and maintaining a strong sense of purpose and leadership, anyone can achieve their goals and create a lasting legacy.

What have you learned from Ray Croc, the man behind the success of McDonald?

His story is one of perseverance, hard work, and innovation. From humble beginnings, he turned a single restaurant into a global business, changing the fast-food industry forever. Every businessman or woman today can learn from his determination and his ability to adapt to changing times.

How has that motivated you?

CONCLUSION

Discovering your passion and purpose is important for personal and business growth. When you're truly passionate about something, it never feels like work. It's an activity you're excited to do, and you're always looking for ways to improve and learn more about it. This is why it's essential to find your passion if you're looking to move forward in your career, in business and life in general.

Finding your passion and purpose is a journey that requires self-reflection and exploration. But once you find it, you'll be more fulfilled and motivated to achieve your goals and succeed in your career. The first step to discovering your passion is to ask yourself what brings you joy and fulfillment. What are the things that you enjoy doing, and what makes you happy? Think about your hobbies, the things you do in your spare time, and the things you love talking about. These are all great starting points to help identify your passion.

Next, think about how you can translate your passion into a career. What are the skills and knowledge that you need to develop to pursue your passion professionally? Research different industries and job roles to find the ones that align with your passion and skills.

Your passion may not necessarily align with your current job, and that's okay. It's never too late to make a change and pursue your passion. Take small steps towards your goal, such as taking courses or volunteering in your desired industry, to gain experience and build your network.

We have also been able to establish that owning a business can be a truly fulfilling and rewarding experience. It is better than working for someone, especially where your talents can't be put into full use or you do not enjoy a good pay and freedom to attend to other needs of life.

While running your business may entail a lot of hard work, dedication, and commitment, the benefits are worth it. Being your own boss gives you the freedom to make your own decisions, set your own schedule, and work on projects that you are passionate about.

You have the flexibility to create a work-life balance that suits you, and you can choose who you work with and how you work with them. Moreover, owning a business can be financially rewarding, as you have the potential to earn more than what you would as an employee. You have the ability to build equity in your business and create a valuable asset that you can sell in the future. It also gives a sense of pride and accomplishment as you see your hard work and efforts come to fruition.

Owning a business can be an exciting and empowering experience. It allows you to take control of your future and pursue something that you are truly passionate about. So, if you have an entrepreneurial spirit and a desire to create something of your own, don't be afraid to take the leap and start your own business. The rewards will be worth it.

Having a mentor for your business is vital if you desire success. It can provide you with numerous benefits that can help you navigate the complexities of running a business. One of the most significant benefits of having a mentor as discussed in this book is access to their experience and knowledge. An experienced mentor can provide you with valuable insights and guidance based on years of experience in the industry. They can also help you avoid common mistakes and pitfalls that they may have encountered in their own business journey.

An alternative to mentorship is having a partner who you share ideas with. collaborating with partners is a win-win situation for everyone involved. By sharing ideas, knowledge and experience, you can all benefit and grow your businesses together.

Then, in running your business, never make use of workers who lack the needed skills and passion to drive your business to the next phase. Having highly skilled and passionate workers in your business. Invest in them. When you invest in your employees and provide them with opportunities to grow and develop their skills, you create a workforce that is dedicated, motivated, and committed to your company's success. The power of passion and skill cannot be underestimated. You must prioritize these traits when hiring and evaluating your team members.

But how do you identify your passion to prepare for this transition?

Positive thinking and optimism are both necessary qualities to soar in business. It's easy to fall into a negative mindset and become discouraged when things don't go as planned with your business. However, having a positive attitude and optimistic outlook can help you stay motivated, overcome obstacles, and achieve your goals. Remember that optimism is a choice, and with practice, you can train your mind to think positively even in challenging situations if you truly have passion for that business.

Finally, passion is a powerful force that drives success. It creates a positive work culture, increases productivity, and fosters innovation and creativity. Employers should strive to attract and retain passionate employees as they are essential to the success and growth of any business. If you want to become a successful businessman or woman, invest in what you love -your passion, nurture and retain highly skilled and passionate workers. With these, you can build a strong and successful team that will help your business thrive.

ALSO FROM THE AUTHOR

The Ghost Writer
coming soon

'The Ghost Writer' a Romantic Thriller full of mystery that keeps you hooked on, an absolute page turner.
……..*His life will never be the same after this.*

ABOUT THE AUTHOR

My name is Martin van Helden (post grad MBA) Author of amazing business books and (Romantic) Thrillers.

My long history of owning several businesses, Doing a lot of research and traveling all over the world has given me the unique

Opportunity to write these amazing educating and entertaining books.

Martin has a way writing to simplifying complex material into an easy read and he has a deep passion for businesses / accounting and (thriller) mysteries with a certain depth in the storyline, and he has written other compelling books.

He likes these books to be a base and encouragement for people to get the best out of life and their business.

Martin likes people to use the solutions in the books as a LEGO type system to form your own solution and optimizing the usage of these books.

https://martinvheldenmvh.wixsite.com/author-martin-van-he

Milton Keynes UK
Ingram Content Group UK Ltd.
UKHW020801241123
433194UK00016B/1048